ABOUT OMEGA

Omega was founded in 1977 at a time when holistic health, psychological inquiry, world music and art, meditation, and new forms of spiritual practice were just budding in American culture. Omega was then just a small band of seekers searching for new answers to perennial questions about human health and happiness. The mission was as simple as it was large: to look everywhere for the most effective strategies and inspiring traditions that might help people bring more meaning and vitality into their lives.

Since then, Omega has become the nation's largest holistic learning center. Every year more than 25,000 people attend workshops, retreats, and conferences in health, psychology, the arts, and spirituality on its eighty-acre campus in the countryside of Rhinebeck, New York, and at other sites around the country. While Omega has grown in size, its mission remains the same. Omega is not aligned with any particular healing method or spiritual tradition. Its programs feature all of the world's wisdom traditions and are committed to offering people an opportunity to explore their own path to better health, personal growth, and inner peace.

The name Omega was inspired by the writings of Teilhard de Chardin, a twentieth-century mystic and philosopher who used the word to describe the point within each one of us where our inner spiritual nature meets our outer worldly nature. Teilhard believed that the synthesis of these two domains presented the greatest challenge—and the greatest hope—for human evolution. Of this belief in the balance between world and spirit, Teilhard wrote, "I am going to broadcast the seed and let the wind carry it where it will."

Omega has taken on the task of helping spread that seed so that a better world for all of us can continue to take root and grow.

OMEGA
Institute for Holistic Studies

D1501874

The Omega Institute
Mind, Body, Spirit Series

The Essentials of Yoga
Vitality and Wellness
Writing Your Authentic Self

AND COMING SOON . . .

Contemplative Living
Bodywork Basics
The Power of Ritual

An Omega Institute Mind, Body, Spirit Book

The Essentials of Yoga

Dinabandhu Sarley

and

Ila Sarley

A DELL TRADE PAPERBACK

A DELL TRADE PAPERBACK

Published by
Dell Publishing
a division of
Random House, Inc.
1540 Broadway
New York, New York 10036

Written by: Sarah Priestman
Series Consulting Editor: Robert Welsch
Series Editor: Kathleen Jayes
Series Manager: James Kullander
Illustrations by: Howard R. Roberts (HROBERTSD@aol.com)
Literary Representative: Ling Lucas, Nine Muses and Apollo Inc.

Dell books may be purchased for business or promotional use or for special
sales. For information please write to: Special Markets Department, Random
House, Inc., 1540 Broadway, New York, N.Y. 10036

DTP and the colophon are trademarks of Random House, Inc.

Library of Congress Cataloging in Publication Data
Sarley, Ila.
    The essentials of yoga / Ila Sarley and Dinabandhu Sarley.
        p.   cm.—(The Omega Institute mind, body, spirit series)
    Includes bibliographical references and index.
    ISBN 0-440-50873-8
    I. Yoga, Hatha.   I. Sarley, Dinabandhu.   II. Omega Institute.
III. Title.   IV. Series.
RA781.7.S264   1999
613.7'046—dc21   99-25039
                                                                    CIP

Printed in the United States of America
Published simultaneously in Canada
September 1999

10   9   8   7   6   5   4   3   2   I

RRD

BOOK DESIGN BY JENNIFER ANN DADDIO

Omega Institute sends out heartfelt thanks and appreciation to staff members and teachers for their support and contribution in the preparation and publishing of this book.

Contents

Introduction

When we first opened our doors at Omega Institute in 1977, we envisioned a place of learning, of community, and of spirit. We didn't know if our enthusiasm would reach those who read our initial—and in those days, tiny—brochures. In the early days, we never knew if anyone would come to the workshops that we hosted on holistic health, self-development, spiritual understanding, and the arts.

But people did come. Year after year, first to a handful of classes at one small center and now, more than twenty years later, to hundreds of offerings at our home campus in Rhinebeck, New York, and conferences in cities around the country.

In the early days, people came to Omega because they wanted a deeper understanding of the world, a healthier outlook on themselves, and more joy and compassion in their lives. These reasons still hold true today.

When we create a schedule of workshops and programs to respond to these needs, the study of yoga is always among the most important—and popular—that we offer. It's been this way since the beginning. Some of yoga's greatest contemporary teachers have joined our faculty, including Swami Sri Satchidananda and Yogi Amrit Desai. Lilias Folan, whose PBS show introduced millions of people to the practice; Phoenix Rising Therapy founder Michael Lee; Joan White, a renowned Inyengar yoga teacher, and Sanskrit scholar Kofi Busia have all taught with us for years. Beryl Bender and Thom Birch, pioneers of Astanga yoga in the United States, are also longtime Omega faculty and friends.

Yoga is woven into the Omega experience even for those attending workshops that have nothing to do with the subject. We offer all attendees the opportunity to take optional yoga classes on a drop-in basis at our campus and conferences. This is because we know how important it is to stay in tune with the body and spirit, especially when participating in a learning environment as energizing and creative as Omega's. We feel that giving our participants the chance to relax and reenergize in a yoga class supports their overall learning experience.

Omega recently broadened its commitment to yoga—and to bringing yoga out into the world—by offering a teachers' certification program. Over the last few years hundreds of students have spent an intensive training period on campus, and many are now teaching on their own.

Think back to where you were in 1977—Omega's first summer. Perhaps you were just finishing college, or starting your family, or in the middle of your working career. Try to remember where you lived, who your closest friends were, the things you did in your spare time. Now imagine yourself buying a book on yoga at that time in your life. Would you have been interested in the subject? If so, would you have told anybody?

For many people, yoga was considered "fringe" back then, but at Omega it was already becoming one of our most popular programs. Yoga has always been an integral part of holistic education at Omega and a key resource for people who wanted to become more fit, or explore the body-mind connection, or to reduce stress in their lives. Now, as yoga becomes more commonplace and accessible, we will continue to offer programs with the finest teachers.

This book is written with the same intentions with which we opened the doors of Omega: learning, community, and spirit. It is designed to give you a friendly, comprehensive overview both of the practice of yoga and of the body-mind connection that is inherent to its study. Enjoy!

What Is Yoga?

Have you noticed how yoga seems to be turning up everywhere these days? Chances are, if you chose this book in a bookstore, it probably came off a shelf that held a number of titles on the subject. Your health club may have just expanded the numbers of classes it offers, or you may have noticed that you keep running into people—at work, or through friends—who say they're trying yoga, and everybody you talk to is enthusiastic about their experience.

In the past few years, new yoga studios have opened their doors in big cities and small towns across the United States. In fact, when the editors at *Yoga Journal* recently commissioned the Roper Poll to do a nationwide survey of people's thoughts about yoga, they discovered that 6 million Americans practice regularly. An additional 16 million people expressed an interest in taking a class. This means that if you are just beginning to explore yoga, you are not alone.

Yoga is not only a staple offering in wellness spas and fitness centers. Now even corporate retreat centers offer attendees yoga sessions to start the day. Classes ori-

"The seeker who sets out upon the way shines bright over the world."
—THE DHAMMAPADA (SAYINGS OF THE BUDDHA)

> "Hatha yoga is based on the principle that changes in consciousness can be brought about by setting in motion currents of certain kinds of subtler forces in the physical body."
>
> —I. K. TAIMNI

ented to specific needs have emerged, as well, such as prenatal and postnatal yoga and sessions designed for people recovering from cancer or other illnesses.

For all the attention yoga is getting, and all the images one might bring to it—such as people contorted into astounding pretzellike shapes, swamis in flowing robes, or leotard-clad models on instructional video boxes—yoga is actually a straightforward endeavor.

Anyone can practice yoga. Age doesn't matter, nor does physical conditioning. Anytime is the right time to begin. All you need is your body, a small amount of space, and a desire for a healthier, more fulfilling life.

Yoga is not as mysterious as it seems. It is not a religion, though many people do find spiritual guidance in its practice and teachings. It is also not a sport, though it does build endurance and strengthen the body. If you are looking for a challenging physical workout, some schools offer this, but many offer an easy, gentle practice.

Essentially, yoga is a system of physical and mental exercises designed to balance and unite the mind, body, and spirit. In Sanskrit, yoga is most commonly defined as

> "Yoga is first and foremost the discipline of conscious living. When we take charge of our lives, we also tap into our inner potential for happiness, or what in Sanskrit is called ananda. This primal joy, which transcends the ego or personality, wells up in our hearts and infuses our whole being with vibrant energy—life. Thus energized, or enlivened, we can go about the business of our daily living in a harmonious manner. We become highly creative, establishing order where there is chaos, instilling life where there is a vacuum, causing comfort where there is distress. In other words, because we are full of joy and life, we become a healing presence in the world."
>
> —GEORG FEUERSTEIN, STEPHAN BODAIN, WITH THE STAFF OF
> *YOGA JOURNAL, LIVING YOGA: A COMPREHENSIVE GUIDE FOR DAILY LIFE*

"union, joining together." In fact, the Sanskrit root word, *yuj*, means "yoke," such as yokin, or connecting things.

Yoga is also about the person practicing it, as it works differently for different people, depending on what you bring to it. It is simple, it is subtle, and it can be joyous.

People are drawn to yoga because of its benefits, which can be felt soon after one begins. It strengthens and tones the muscles, reduces stress, teaches relaxation, and just plain feels good.

At first yoga might look like plain old stretching, so you may wonder what makes it different from warm-up exercises people do before jogging. The difference has to do with the intention and experience. Exercise is goal-oriented. The goal could be to finish a routine, or flatten the belly, or lift a certain number of weights, but in each case it is usually to accomplish what you are doing and move on to the next thing.

Yoga, on the other hand, is process-oriented. The idea is to focus awareness on exactly what you are doing, in the moment. Yoga coordinates breath with movement, allowing you to sink into the experience of a stretch rather than simply finishing it in

What's that word? If you come across a term or a phrase in bold, that means it is included in the glossary in the back of this book.

order to go for a run. Yoga not only stretches and tones the body, it also teaches the practitioner to be more present while doing so.

There is a component of yoga that is goal-oriented, as making progress through the levels of postures can be an important part of the practice. But it isn't the primary focus—in fact, you progress more easily in yoga when you are aware of the postures that are appropriate for your own level.

"Awareness changes how we physically move. As we become more fluid and resilient so do the mental, emotional, and spiritual movements of our lives."

—EMILE CONRAD DA'OUD

Some people prefer yoga rather than spending an hour with weight machines or in an aerobics class because it provides a nurturing time-out from a busy day. On the days when your life feels like it's bursting at the seams, the peace and quiet of a yoga class can be an oasis. It's dependable, too, because you know you'll walk out feeling refreshed. Some classes are also a form of community. Though the practice itself is inner-directed, many beginner classes have a we're-starting-out-together feeling of camaraderie. You may develop friendships with other class members, as you are all learning and exploring together.

There's another aspect that keeps people coming to yoga, as well, which has to do with its connection to emotions and spirituality. Even as a beginner, you may experience a feeling of serenity at the end of the class. By practicing breathing techniques and moving through a variety of postures, you will have awakened your nervous system and energized your body. Classes end with deep relaxation, which leaves you feeling both calm and rejuvenated.

As you continue practicing, you may find that yoga can lead you on a journey into yourself. You may find the link between the body, mind, and spirit to offer a new arena of inner growth and self-understanding. People who are drawn to yoga for its health benefits often become more deeply involved once they discover its uncanny ability to promote emotional balance and spiritual awareness.

A Brief History

Yoga may be new to your health club, but it has been around for thousands of years. It is included in the oldest known text in the world, the **Rig-Veda** (meaning "Knowledge of Praise"), which is estimated to have originated in India 4,000 years ago. The Rig-Veda is a collection of 1,028 hymns composed in archaic Sanskrit that were memorized and passed down by oral tradition up until a few hundred years ago.

"Yoga is the stilling of the restlessness of the mind."

—YOGA SUTRAS

Indian stone sculptures from as early as 3,000 B.C. also demonstrate yoga postures. Yoga shows up 500 years later in Hindu scriptures called the *Vedas*, and again in the Indian epic poem **Bhagavad Gita** in 500 B.C.

The first systemized treatise devoted solely to yoga is called the **Yoga Sutras.** It is said to have been written in 200 B.C. by an Indian sage and physician named Patanjali. Patanjali is considered the father of yoga because, after generations of oral teachings, his texts made it more accessible.

Basically, the Sutras are a collection of 195 statements that explore what it takes to gain mastery over the mind and emotions. They also offer advice on spiritual growth. Many of the teachings you will run across as you study yoga, even in a beginning class, will be based on the philosophical guidelines of this ancient text. Some instructors may refer to a quote from the Sutras to start the class, or mention how a pose relates to the Sutras' teachings.

Yoga Comes to America

To look at the history of yoga in America, we will fast-forward from the time of Patanjali to the turn of the century—or, more specifically, to the 1893 World Parliament of Religions, which took place in Chicago, Illinois. This was the setting in which an Indian yogi, Swami Vivekananda, received a warm reception from a large American audience for his lecture on yoga.

"The ancient yogis had a profound understanding of man's essential nature and of what he needs to live in harmony with himself and his environment. They perceived the physical body as a vehicle, with the mind as the driver, the soul man's true identity, and action, emotion and intelligence as the three forces that pull the body-vehicle. They formulated a unique method for maintaining this balance—a method that combines all the movements you need for physical health with the breathing and meditation techniques that ensure peace of mind."

—*THE SIVANADA COMPANION TO YOGA*

BY THE SIVANADA YOGA CENTER STAFF AND LUCY L. NARAYANI

> "Dwell as near as possible to the channel in which your life flows."
> —HENRY DAVID THOREAU

The impetus for this lecture may have started back in 1877, when the Theosophical Society in New York City was founded by Madame Blavatsky and Colonel Henry Steel Olcott. The society was one of the first to encourage members to study Eastern religion and mystical traditions. Madame Blavatsky published *Isis Unveiled* in 1877 and *The Secret Doctrine* in 1888, both of which explored the teachings of ancient Hindu texts.

Around the same time, Henry David Thoreau and Ralph Waldo Emerson found inspiration in the Bhagavad Gita, a sacred yogic text. They shared their enthusiasm with other followers in a movement known as transcendentalism, which focused on spiritual intuition and self-reliance, and were especially influential with a niche in the Boston area known as the Concord Circle. Other members of the Concord Circle were also captivated by the unusual philosophies of yoga and did their part to make sure that *The Light in Asia*, a biography of Gautama Buddha by Edwin Arnold, was published in 1897. Thus a small group of New Englanders searching for religious meaning laid the groundwork for the acceptance of yoga in America.

A few years after his popular presentation at the World Parliament of Religions, Swami Vivekenanda founded the New York Vedanta Society—and it is still thriving today. It should be noted, however, that the branch of yoga he taught was not **Hatha yoga,** which focuses on exploring postures. Vivekenanda taught **Raja yoga,** which concentrates on meditation and the control of the intellect to attain enlightenment. (The different branches of yoga will be explored later in this chapter.) Therefore, the initial study of yoga in America focused more on the mind and spirit than it did on the body.

Hatha yoga was introduced to America via Long Island, New York, in 1919 by Yogendra Mastamani. His home ashram in India is credited with starting a dialogue with the American alternative medical community to explore the healing aspects of yoga, launching a relationship that still exists today.

In 1920 interest in Hatha yoga began to pick up speed. The International Congress of Religious Liberals hosted the Indian spiritual leader Paramahansa

Yogananda at its conference in Boston, and five years later he founded the Self Realization Fellowship in Los Angeles to further his teachings. The organization still attracts thousands of followers a year. His book, *Autobiography of a Yogi,* was published in 1946 and remains a classic text.

Next stop, Hollywood. In 1947 Russian-born Indra Devi opened a studio to teach Hatha yoga and found a strong following in the stars of stage and screen. Among those exploring the union of body, mind, and spirit were Jennifer Jones, Gloria Swanson, and Robert Ryan. Indra Devi's audience went beyond celebrities, however, and her influence on making yoga more familiar in the American landscape earned her the title "First Lady of Yoga."

Though yoga may have been familiar to some, we have television to thank for making it accessible to all. In 1961 Richard Hittleman switched from the yoga stu-

Lilias Folan, an Omega faculty member, recalls bringing yoga to the airwaves in the early 1970s. "Those were the days when yoga was still considered to be on the fringe," she says. "The camera people, who were all men then, were all bored with it. They thought nothing was happening. It was not considered fresh and interesting like it is now. One time I asked the producer why he spent so much time with one camera shot," she remembers, "and he said, 'Lilias, I didn't know if you were going to levitate.' I also received letters from all over the country, and even from churches in my own hometown, saying that yoga was a religion and shouldn't be on public television."

Folan felt the need to persevere despite the misunderstandings. "I felt I had no choice," she explains. "I'm actually a shy person, so it wasn't easy, but I felt a need to communicate about it.

"I didn't realize this then," Folan says, "but when I look back now I see that I was in the process of reconnecting with my spirit during that time. As you get stronger in your inner connection, which yoga was helping me to do even as I was in the midst of getting the word out about it, there is nothing that can take you from the place of your own strength."

Folan sees yoga's current popularity as just one aspect of the growing awareness of spiritual and physical health. "I am especially happy about people beginning their practice at midlife," she says. "People used to think it was too difficult to start the practice at this age, but it is actually the best time."

dio to the broadcast studio. He was the first to offer yoga over the airwaves, followed ten years later by Lilias Folan's series on public television. Folan filmed 500 different shows, some of which are still in reruns and draw a large viewership.

Current Trends

Recent decades, of course, have witnessed an explosion in yoga's popularity. As the interest in Eastern spirituality and health took hold in the 1960s and 1970s, yoga became a natural vehicle for many. A number of residential communities based on yoga principles emerged, offering the opportunity to immerse one's entire life in the practice. By the end of the 1970s, several such communities were thriving—the Kripalu Center in Lenox, Massachusetts; Mt. Madonna in Santa Cruz, California; and Yogaville in Buckingham, Virginia, for example—each promoting a devotional lifestyle.

By the 1980s the fitness craze was rocking America. Health centers popped up overnight, as the industry became a multimillion-dollar business. Aerobics became the "in thing." Unfortunately, many Americans who started out dancing—or running, or lifting weights—soon found themselves sitting, and often in their doctors' waiting room. Studies showed that 75 percent of aerobics instructors and 45 percent of participants sustained some type of injury from exercise.

The result of all the 1980s' excess has been a more careful approach to fitness in the 1990s. In many cases, aerobics has been modified to include a low-impact approach, and "no pain, no gain" is now "easy does it." This shift in attitude in the fit-

---

"Rather than some kind of dogged pushing through, strong determination involves connecting with joy, relaxing, and trusting. It's determination to use every challenge you meet as an opportunity to open your heart and soften, determination not to withdraw. One simple way to develop this strength is to develop a strong-hearted spiritual practice."

—PEMA CHODRON

ness movement has also contributed to the boom in yoga. Health and fitness centers now are often a great resource for yoga classes, especially for beginners.

Yoga has also grown more popular because of preventive medicine, whose philosophy invites individuals to take responsibility for their own wellness through diet, exercise, and maintaining a balanced lifestyle. As people attempt to manage their own health, they often try a class.

Today yoga is accessible to almost everyone. You can use your library card to check out a yoga video featuring Jane Fonda or Ali MacGraw, or you can join a class at the local community center. You can vacation at a yoga retreat in the Caribbean. If you are just beginning yoga, the fact that it has recently gained in popularity means you will have more choices—and you can rest assured that its increased availability does not dilute its strength.

Despite the rise and fall of its popularity and prevalence, yoga itself has not changed over the course of time. The postures, breathing exercises, and meditation techniques remain the same, as do their goal: to create a unity between body, mind, and spirit. This doesn't change, no matter where or when yoga is practiced.

Branches of Yoga

The method of using postures and the breath is only one way—or branch—of practicing yoga.

When you were a child, did you have a favorite tree to climb? If so, you may remember the experience of trying out different branches as you made your way up. You may recall how closely a branch grew to the ground, allowing you to hoist yourself up easily, or whether a higher branch felt sturdy under your weight as you shimmied along it, hoping for a bird's-eye view of your own backyard.

In ancient times, yoga was thought of as a tree. It was considered alive, and growing, and the different facets of its practice were considered to be branches—living and expanding as part of the tree. To learn about the different approaches to yoga, allow yourself to imagine the tree from your childhood, complete with roots, branches, limbs, blossoms, and fruit.

The distinct branches of yoga each represent a particular approach to life. And just as climbing a real tree means you might try every branch or select a favorite route and use it over and over again, the different branches of yoga can be used at different times, for different reasons, or you can stick to just one. They each contribute to the strength and beauty of the tree that is yoga.

Hatha Yoga

This is the most popular branch. When people say they are taking a yoga class, they usually mean they are learning the poses (or **asanas,** which is the Sanskrit word for postures or exercises) and breathing techniques of Hatha yoga. At the same time, Hatha yoga is taught in a number of styles, so one Hatha yoga class can be very different from another. The various schools of Hatha yoga are covered in Chapter 3.

People are attracted to this branch because of its benefits: It tones the body, stills the mind, and creates a feeling of relaxation. The breathing exercises one learns, and the ability to calm the mind, can be transferred into other areas of life to reduce stress and increase one's ability to "be here now."

When literally translated, *hatha* means "power," or "effort," which reflects the intention of controlling the body. The word can also be understood to mean "complementary forces," as *ha* translates into "sun," and *tha* to moon.

The duality of sun and moon—or of bringing any opposites into balance—is at the root of Hatha yoga. As you begin to practice, you will discover that each expansion is met with a contraction and that a twist of the spine in one direction is followed by a turn to the opposite side. Postures that offer an equal workout to both sides of the body are one way in which Hatha yoga brings opposites into balance.

Hatha yoga also balances the body and mind. This occurs not only by the feel-good sensation of exercises and relaxation but also because whenever we teach our bodies to move in new ways, the mind is being trained, as well. Here are some examples.

FLEXIBILITY

The postures in Hatha yoga stretch the muscles, ease the joints, and help to create a limber body. Some beginners discover that when the body moves with more fluidity, their thoughts tend to flow more smoothly as well.

STRENGTH AND ENDURANCE

Hatha yoga tones muscle groups through the postures, enhancing stamina and endurance. The combination of feeling more in shape, focusing the mind, and breathing properly also strengthens the inner self. In this way, practicing yoga may remind novices of times when they have been involved in other physical activities—from hiking or tennis to organized sports. Just getting the body moving again can lift people's spirits and shift perspective.

AWARENESS

Awareness is sharpened in Hatha yoga because the process of learning and practicing postures involves concentration. This concentration may then shift to other areas of our lives, increasing the ability to be present and aware.

"The underlying purpose of the different aspects of the practice of yoga is to reunite the individual self with the Absolute or pure consciousness."

—*THE SIVANADA COMPANION TO YOGA*

BY THE SIVANADA YOGA CENTER STAFF AND LUCY L. NARAYANI

Though Hatha yoga is the branch most beginners are familiar with, there are more ways to explore this tree called yoga.

Karma Yoga

Have you ever seen the bumper sticker that reads "My karma ran over my dogma"? Once you get a feel for the meaning of **Karma yoga,** you might think the bumper sticker is announcing good news.

Followers of Karma yoga believe that what goes around comes around. It is based on the principle that what we experience today is a product of our past actions. There is not good karma or bad karma, as it is simply a belief in the way things work. It is similar to the law of cause and effect. This suggests that to ensure a good future, our current behaviors need to be positive. Followers of Karma yoga are committed to self-less service, as by serving others they are working toward—and sometimes already ex-periencing—enlightenment.

People do not have to consciously follow Karma yoga to be practicing the branch. Whenever we volunteer our services to help a greater good or approach our work and treat others in a selfless manner, we are practicing Karma yoga.

Bhakti Yoga

Students of this branch follow a path of the heart, as **Bhakti yoga** places devotion to the Divine ahead of everything else. Bhakti yoga is a positive way of channeling emo-tions and nurtures acceptance and tolerance of everyone we come in contact with. Distracted minds and the quandaries of a material world dissolve through the au-thentic experience of love and reverence for all of life.

Though Bhakti yoga may sound like it is limited to a life cloistered from the harsh realities of the modern world, some of the world's most powerful leaders have di-

---

"People think love is an emotion. Love is good sense."

—KEN KESEY

Karma and Bhakti Yoga—Two Wings of One Bird

At first glance these two schools of yoga may seem interchangeable. They are quite close, so here's another way of understanding them.

Karma yoga is about working for the greater good of society. Though there is the idea of creating "good karma," the foundation of Karma yoga is based more on an attitude of spirit in action than on an accumulation of spiritual points. In this way, the "union" of yoga is experienced through one's personal connection to service.

According to Yogi Amrit Desai, the founder of the Kripalu Yoga Center, "Work performed with the right attitude is worship in action. When you learn to work with love, your life will be an expression of joy."

All work performed with a selfless, serving attitude reflects the path of Karma yoga, but certain areas of work may lend themselves to cultivating this attitude more than others. These areas include working with people who are sick or poor.

Bhakti yoga, on the other hand, reveals the interconnectedness that is at the root of yoga through an all-pervasive, and also very authentic, sense of love. It suggests that the experience we feel when we are "in love" is available to us at all times, regardless of the existence of a romantic partner—that in fact, this experience of love is a basic fact of life—when we are available to it.

"Our natural state, prior to the appearance of the individuated body-mind, is one of love and bliss," writes Georg Feuerstein et al. "Our feelings of personal love, compassion, empathy, reverence, and devotion are manifestations of that deeper love-bliss. Bhakti yoga makes use of these positive human emotions, to help us awaken to our true identity and recover the original love-bliss. It seeks to refine them until our ability to love extends into infinity."

Bhakti yoga recognizes the essence of love in the interconnectedness of all living things, so it is brought to life in ecological and service work. Many faith-oriented service projects are based on the same kind of thinking that is at the core of Bhakti yoga, as well.

rected their intentions through Bhakti philosophies. Mahatma Gandhi, Martin Luther
King, Jr., and Mother Teresa are all examples of Bhakti yoga coming to life.

Jnana Yoga

When inquiring minds need to know, they turn to **Jnana yoga.** Students of Jnana
yoga tap into their inner knowledge through self-inquiry, meditation, and contemplation. The goal is beyond a gathering of information, however, and toward a clarity of
what is deception and what is truth.

The inquiry process is the tool used to shift perception, working toward the moment when people move beyond the type of knowledge accumulated through the intellect and into the direct experience of the self. In this way, Jnana yoga provides direct
knowledge of the divine.

Tantra Yoga

Did you skip ahead to this branch when you saw the title on the page, hoping to finally get the inside scoop on "bedroom yoga"? Many people think that **Tantra yoga**

is all about sex, but it just isn't true. Tantra is the path of ritual, and since one of the rituals it includes is sacred sexuality, a number of people have focused on this aspect. In fact, most tantric schools actually recommend a celibate lifestyle.

The tantric practice cultivates a reverential attitude toward life, and practitioners experience the Divine in all actions. Students of Tantra are drawn to customs and rituals as a way of honoring the spirit in all of life. This is true for any rites of passage, such as birthdays, anniversaries, or holidays, and all types of ceremony, whether it is the consecration of the Eucharist or a Japanese tea ceremony, as they are all opportunities to experience union with the life force. In this way, the consecration of a relationship is also a sacred ritual, and thus students of Tantra emphasize the divine nature of sexuality.

Remember, just as the different branches of the tree you explored as a child were useful for taking you different ways on your climbing journey, so the different branches of yoga can all be part of your path. Each one will lead you closer to the feeling of union with the greater life force.

Welcome to Yoga

Now that you know something about what yoga is, where it came from, and the different ways to practice it, perhaps you are ready to join a class. If so, this book is organized to help you along the way.

The next chapter takes the broadly stated benefits and boils them down to specifics, exploring the physiological connection between stress reduction and yoga and citing studies that demonstrate yoga's impact on health. In Chapter 3, the various schools of Hatha yoga are explained, so you will know what to choose from as you begin your practice. Chapter 4 looks more deeply at the body-mind connection,

"Turning the attention to the body is the beginning of
the process of compassionate self-care."
—STEPHEN R. SCHWARTZ

Chapter 5 describes the role of breath in the practice, and Chapters 6 through 8 offer detailed descriptions and illustrations of postures geared to the beginning student. Chapter 9 provides a list of suggested routines geared for different schedules. The last two chapters are designed to support you in developing your own path as you journey into yoga, as they offer an exploration of diet, meditation, spirituality, and community.

Yoga is a satisfying, fun activity that can produce powerful results. It is more than just movement, because it can wake up your body, hone your mind, and energize your spirit. It links the body, mind, and spirit, so you will discover the inevitable connection between what you learn about yourself on the mat and how these lessons are incorporated into everyday life.

As you begin to study yoga, remember that your experience may change, depend-

---

"Hatha yoga, as the Sanskrit name suggests, is the 'powerful' path of realization. It seeks to awaken the body's inherent psychospiritual energy (called **kundalini**), which is thought to strengthen, heal, rejuvenate and supercharge our physical frame. The reasoning behind this approach is that the advanced practices of yoga, such as meditation and ecstasy, require a strong and healthy body.
"Adepts at yoga have demonstrated incredible control over their bodies. As laboratory tests bear out, they can stop their hearts, enter into a state of suspended animation, and regulate their brain waves at will. But astonishing as these feats are, they are not important in themselves. Rather they suggest that the great masters of yoga have access to a level of consciousness that is closed to most other people. They are in touch with the hidden dimension of existence, which, they assure us, is far richer, more joyous, and more rewarding than the experiences of ordinary life.
"They also tell us that everyone can gain access to that same level of reality, providing they diligently apply themselves to the practice of yoga. Clearly, the path is a lifelong endeavor, but this should encourage rather than discourage us. For we do not need to be in a big hurry. As the scriptures of yoga affirm, no effort is lost on the path. However, we must be willing to make the first step, then the next, then the next."
—GEORG FEUERSTEIN, STEPHAN BODIAN, WITH THE STAFF OF *YOGA JOURNAL*,
LIVING YOGA: A COMPREHENSIVE GUIDE FOR DAILY LIFE

---

ing on the kinds of thoughts and feelings you bring to the practice. In this way, yoga is about you, and your practice will both reflect and respond to your needs.

Yoga is also about the connection between who you are and the rest of the world. Ultimately, the union that is yoga is felt as a "oneness" with the world. Even as a beginner, you may have a fleeting moment where this connection is felt. In yoga, this is considered an experience of the true self, and it is the goal of yoga practitioners everywhere.

SUGGESTED READING

Budilovsky, Joan, and Adamson, Eve. *The Complete Idiot's Guide to Yoga.* New York: Macmillan, 1997.

Carrico, Mara. *Yoga Journal's Yoga Basics.* New York: Holt, 1997.

Christensen, Alice. *The American Yoga Association Beginner's Manual.* New York: Simon & Schuster, 1987.

Devereux, Godfrey. *The Elements of Yoga.* Rockport, Mass.: Element Books, 1997.

Dworkis, Sam, with Moline, Peg. *ExTension: The 20-Minute-a-Day Yoga-Based Program to Relax, Release, and Rejuvenate the Average Stressed-Out Over-35-Year-Old Body.* New York: Poseidon, 1994.

Feuerstein, Georg, Bodian, Stephan, with the staff of *Yoga Journal. Living Yoga: A Comprehensive Guide for Daily Life.* New York: Jeremy P. Tarcher, 1993.

Feuerstein, Georg. *The Shambhala Guide to Yoga.* Boston: Shambhala, 1996.

Hewitt, James. *The Complete Yoga Book: Yoga of Breathing, Yoga of Posture, and Yoga of Meditation.* New York: Schocken Books, 1990.

Integral Yoga Institute. *The Dictionary of Sanskrit Names.* Yogaville, Va.: Integral Yoga Publications, 1989.

Iyengar, B. K. S. *Light on the Yoga Sutras of Patanjali: Patanjala Yoga Pradipika.* United Kingdom: Aquarian Press, 1993.

Kent, Howard. *Yoga Made Easy: A Personal Yoga Program That Will Transform Your Daily Life.* Allentown, Pa.: People's Medical Society, 1994.

McClure, Vimala. *A Woman's Guide to Tantra Yoga.* Novato, Ca.: New World Library, 1997.

Miller, Barbara S. (trans.). *Yoga: Discipline of Freedom: The Yoga Sutra Attributed to Patanjali.* Berkeley: University of California Press, 1996.

Mishra, Rammurti S. *Yoga Sutras: The Textbook of Yoga Psychology.* Garden City, N.Y.: Anchor, 1963.

Prakash, Prem. *The Yoga of Spiritual Devotion: A Modern Translation of the Narada Bhakti Sutras.* Rochester, Vt.: Inner Traditions International, 1998.

Satchidananda, Sri Swami. *Integral Yoga: The Yoga Sutras of Patanjali.* Pomfret Center, Conn.: Integral Yoga, 1998.

Schiffmann, Erich. *Yoga: The Spirit and Practice of Moving Into Stillness.* New York: Pocket Books, 1996.

Taimni, I. K. *The Science of Yoga: A Commentary on the Yoga Sutras of Patanjali in the Light of Modern Thought.* Madras: Theosophical Publishing House, 1965.

Zebroff, Kareen. *Yoga for Everyone.* Foulsham and Co., 1995.

If you are a beginning student, you may also want to subscribe to *Yoga Journal*—it's got great information and resources. Contact:

Yoga Journal
2054 University Ave., Suite 600
Berkeley, CA 94704
1-800-359-YOGA

The Benefits of Yoga

2

Even if you're new to yoga, chances are you've already heard something about its benefits. Yoga is a systemwide workout. Ask anybody who practices yoga what he or she gets out of it, and you'll probably hear, "It just feels fantastic." That's because it calms the central nervous system, enhances flexibility, and increases strength, vitality, and energy.

Yoga is known for deep relaxation, which eases tension and lowers stress. It tones muscles and joints, which even beginners can feel right away. Yoga helps to improve the body's metabolism, and many of the postures gently massage your internal organs, which helps to stimulate digestion.

Yoga promotes spiritual and psychological health, as well. Simply giving yourself the time to do yoga—to relax into the delicious stretches, to learn the simple breathing and focusing techniques, and to acquaint yourself with the gentle, calm feeling of inner stillness that accompanies the practice—will have a positive influence on your general outlook.

"Life loves to be taken by the lapel and told, 'I'm with you kid. Let's go.'"
—MAYA ANGELOU

Another thing about yoga is that you can experience its benefits no matter how old you are when you first start to practice. Yoga can ease the inertia and stiffness associated with aging. "Yoga exercises reverse the aging process by moving each joint in the body through its full range of motion—stretching, strengthening and balancing each part," writes Suza Francina in *The New Yoga for People Over 50*. "Older students who attend class regularly for at least six months report that their increased strength and range of movement enables them to return to physical activities they thought they had lost forever." These include gardening, climbing stairs, biking, and dancing.

In fact, according to the yogic tradition, beginners who come to yoga in later years are at an ideal age for physiological and spiritual growth. "The practice of yoga not only restores health and vitality of the body, but the philosophy behind yoga is to open and expand a human being on all levels so that aging can become a time of greater perspective and illumination," Francina explains.

Though the pluses of yoga are widely celebrated—no matter when you start—it's only fair to say that not all beginners warm up to yoga right away. If there's something about the practice that feels uncomfortable, you are not alone—but there is a great payoff if you're willing to give it a little time.

That's what Christine Morton, a school librarian who joined a five-day yoga retreat at Omega Institute after several years of weekly classes, recalls from her experience as a beginner. "I never wanted to go to class when I first began," she said, "because the last thing I wanted was something else I 'had' to do."

This soon changed, however. "I began to see that at the end of every class I would feel better. Even if I was at the end of my rope when I walked in, I was feeling calm and energized after an hour.

"Basically, yoga gave me my evenings back," Morton said. "Now I have the energy to go out and do things. Not even a cup of coffee can do that."

Lynn Parker, a business owner in Seattle, Washington, and a mother of three, registered for her first yoga class in her early forties. Her experience as a beginner is also common—she loved it.

"My doctor told me to do it," she explained. "I guess she recognized how much I needed the relaxation and focus that yoga would provide."

"I never expected to feel so good so quickly," she remembers. "The thing that re-

ally struck me is that no matter what space I was in when I went into the class, I came
out feeling calm. I always looked forward to going."

The benefits of yoga may show up in surprising little ways. If you sit at a desk,
yoga can ease and even prevent back pain. It also helps restore muscles injured through
repetitive stress syndrome.

If you're an athlete, you'll find it makes an excellent cross-training system. It improves muscular tone, balance, and coordination. It strengthens muscles that are weak,
stretches those that are tight, and conditions the connective tissue, which can increase
range of motion and help reduce the likelihood of sports-related injuries. The flexibility you'll gain from yoga will also help you recover faster after an aerobic or high-
impact workout.

Yoga is a great beauty secret, as well. After just a few weeks of practicing you'll
stand taller, walk more gracefully, and feel more toned and confident. You'll emanate
well-being. You'll look terrific because you'll feel so good.

Common yoga postures can also relieve mild aches and pains. The Cobra and
Plough alleviate menstrual cramps, and the standing Forward Bend and Bow postures
are good conditioning moves to help relieve lower backaches. The emphasis on breath
work has also been shown to help people with respiratory ailments such as asthma.
And many books that explore a variety of natural approaches to easing the symptoms
of menopause advocate the practice of yoga for its role in reducing tension and enhancing energy.

But there's even more—studies have shown that the benefits of yoga go beyond a fit,
supple body and peace of mind. Because of its deep relaxation and focusing techniques,

yoga works wonders to decrease stress—and managing stress is linked to preventing heart disease, lowering blood pressure, reducing pain, and strengthening the immune system.

Numerous studies have verified the impact relaxation and exercise have in stress reduction. Best known is the work done by Herbert Benson, M.D., and his colleagues at Harvard Medical School in the 1970s and 1980s. They studied what came to be called "the relaxation response," which led to a number of findings on how mind-body mechanisms can be used to influence not only stress but hypertension, heart disease, cancer, and other diseases, as well.

The stress response, which is also known as the fight-or-flight reaction, is the set of physiological changes that get set off in the body when we perceive a challenging or threatening situation.

The stress response is well designed to prepare the body to function at a higher level of efficiency. When the stress is real, this enhances the likelihood of survival. But what's important to remember is that these changes can kick in whether there is something real or not. And the more we appraise the challenge as a threat—even at the subconscious level—the more intense our stress response.

According to Judith Lasater, writing in *Relax and Renew: Restful Yoga for Stressful Times*, "Whatever the stressor, the mind alerts the body that danger is present."

Here's what happens in our bodies—whether we are aware of it or not—when we perceive stress. As Lasater describes, "Heart rate, blood pressure, mental alertness, and muscle tension are increased. The adrenal hormones cause metabolic changes that make energy stores available to each cell and the body begins to sweat. The body also shuts down the systems that are not a priority in the immediacy of the moment, including digestion, elimination, growth, repair and reproduction."

Is all this information about stress making you tense? Here are some easy yoga exercises you can do anytime you are reading or working at your desk to relax your shoulders, neck, and eyes.

NECK AND SHOULDERS

◆ Turkey Stretch

Sit with your spine straight, both feet flat on the floor. Imagine there is a cord attached to the top of your head, and it is gently pulling you to sit up just a little bit taller. Direct your gaze in front of your nose and bring your hand to your chin. Now inhale deeply, resting your hand on your chin. Exhale slowly, gently pressing your chin toward your neck. You should feel this stretch lengthening the back of your neck. Do this three times.

◆ Shoulder Release

Sit with your spine straight, both feet flat on the floor. Keep your arms by your sides, palms turned inward. As you inhale, lift your shoulders up to your earlobes and then exhale, rolling them back down. Go slowly with your breath and movements. Feel your spine lengthen. Repeat five times.

EYES

◆ Eye Calisthenics

Begin by taking in deep inhalations and letting your breath out slowly. Relax your shoulders. Now, keeping your head and shoulders still, inhale slowly and look to the far left. Follow this with a slow exhalation and a look to the far right. Do three full sets, and then blink your eyes for several seconds. Top this off by closing your eyes and taking three long breaths.

◆ Stretch Down to Up

Again, begin with a relaxed, deep breath. Relax your shoulders and rest your hands on your thighs. Keep your shoulders and head still. Slowly inhale, stretching your eyeballs up to-ward the ceiling—or even better, toward the sky. Now exhale, looking down. Do this for three full sets, then close your eyes for three long, gentle breaths.

What does all this have to do with learning yoga? Practicing yoga can help reduce the effect of stress in our lives. Though these physiological changes come in handy when a person is in a life-or-death situation, they can wreak havoc in our day-to-day existence.

First of all, the anxiety of juggling numerous obligations of family, work, relationships, and personal life creates stress. Second, often we can find ourselves in situations that will kick in the physiological response to stress, but we are powerless to act upon it. Think about being stuck in traffic when you know your child is waiting for you to come home. Or being told that a deadline at work was suddenly changed—a project is due a week sooner than you'd planned for—adding to your already over-burdened plate.

These are the kinds of things that activate the stress response. Even more things keep us percolating at a low level of stress every day, day after day. We may think we become accustomed to it, but, in fact, our bodies continue to react with the stress response. We may even begin to accept the racing heart, impatience, and anxiety as normal aspects of everyday life.

Not only are these reactions not normal, they are downright dangerous to your health. If you experience the stress response regularly, and for extended periods of time, these physiological changes can create a cycle of exhaustion in which everything starts to be stressful because you can never catch your breath. This, in turn, can weaken your body's resistance to illness—which can mean you are opening yourself up to serious health consequences.

For example, the stress response has been directly linked to lower immune functioning. In one recent study, 400 healthy volunteers were quarantined for several days and exposed to one of five strains of cold viruses. Subjects reporting high stress levels had over twice the risk of developing colds. Think about your day and the barrage of viruses you come in contact with. Imagine how much your life gets turned upside down when you are laid up in bed for week with a cold and then must play

---

"Learning that we can trust the creative energy of Life itself enables us to relax more and more because we know we don't have to make things happen by the force of our will."

—SWAMI CHETANANANDA

---

catch-up for two weeks once you're on your feet. Feels stressful just to think about it, doesn't it?

Here's where the benefits of yoga are critical to alleviating the wear and tear of stress. Not only does it keep your immune system strong, but the relaxation techniques learned through practicing yoga can also reduce blood pressure, respiratory rate, heart rate, perspiration, muscle tension, and oxygen consumption rate—basically all the physiological reactions that are triggered by stress.

It is important to note that these are the advantages not only of practicing yoga but also of putting meditation, mindfulness, and other techniques that involve centering, focusing, and breath work into your life. In other words, the ways in which yoga works to relax the body and focus the mind are akin to many other relaxation techniques. Because yoga works with the body as well as with the mind, it brings additional perks such as strengthening, balance, and flexibility.

Relaxation training has also been shown to do more than reduce stress. Here are just a few studies demonstrating how the application of relaxation training can positively affect health:

- ✦ Patients with hypertension who took an eight-week training course (and it was only once a week) achieved significantly lower blood pressure—and these benefits were still being maintained three years later.

- ✦ Patients receiving several kinds of elective surgery who were trained in relaxation had fewer experiences of anxiety both before and after surgery, and both the intensity of their pain and their use of medication were reduced.

- ✦ A controlled study of women with premenstrual syndrome (PMS) using the relaxation response twice daily for three months found a 58 percent reduction in the severity of their symptoms.

Studies specific to yoga have proven its unique benefits, as well. According to the University of Texas Lifetime Health Newsletter, "Yoga is gradually becoming more

"Be happy. It's one way of being wise."
—COLETTE

accepted among health care professionals as a tool in the treatment of disease, such as cancer, heart disease, and arthritis. Proven scientific studies have replaced anecdotal evidence and speculation about the effectiveness of yoga in improving blood flow, decreasing heart rate, and enhancing performance of the brain."

For example, yoga was integral in a study that also used exercise, a low-fat diet, and support groups to demonstrate that a healthy lifestyle and behavioral changes could reverse coronary blockages—which is no small feat. Developed by Dr. Dean Ornish, assistant clinical professor of medicine at the University of California, San Francisco, the program showed that 82 percent of the patients who adopted healthier habits—including an hour of yoga every day—had some blockage reversal.

Most interesting to students of yoga is that Ornish's data shows direct correlation between the time spent in yoga practice and a reduction of coronary blockages, which is attributed to the role of yoga in relaxing muscles and reducing stress.

How Long Do I Have to Wait?

Perhaps you are thinking "Okay, these studies are well and good for the person who has been going to classes for a while, but what about me? I'm just starting."

Here's the good news: Yoga is well designed for beginners, because it's possible to feel benefits early on. One study involving women who practiced yoga daily showed a significant change in just four weeks. Their heart and lungs worked more efficiently, and they showed improvement on a treadmill test.

In another study, yoga was shown to improve memory function after less than two weeks. Students who received ten days of training in the practice of yogic breathing showed an average of 84 percent improvement on tests of spatial memory, while their classmates showed no improvement at all.

Some beginners discover experiences that may never show up in a study. Patrice

---

"The only joy in the world is to begin."

—CESARE PAVESE

Lorenz, an elementary school art teacher in New York City, remembers how clearly she recognized the relaxing influence of her first few classes and the surprising way she found her mind connecting things differently within this feeling of calm. "I would start out thinking about the concerns of the day," she explained, "and as the session proceeded I noticed that I was resolving things and making links from one idea to another in a way I never had before. It wasn't as if I was coming up with additional clever ideas, I was just seeing things from a different, more solid perspective. And this was just in the first few classes."

You can trust that soon after you become comfortable with the first few postures and feel familiar with the breathing techniques, you will begin to experience the same kind of wonderful mix of energy and calm that is unique to the practice. For some, this just takes a few classes—or a few sessions at home, poring through a beginner's book and trying out the techniques during a peaceful, quiet time you've set aside just for yourself.

At the same time, the benefits increase in scope and depth as you continue to practice. What at first feels like a new sense of calm will shift into a deeper experience of stillness and serenity as you become more at home with your practice. The initial forays into unfamiliar stretches will soon become long, delightful journeys into deep relaxation as your body becomes more supple and your mind and muscles grow more in sync.

Taking It Off the Mat

The feeling of inner, quiet power that develops from a satisfying yoga practice will begin to be a routine part of your life and will soon show up in your behavior once you're off of the mat and out of your yoga clothes.

This is one of the most compelling benefits of yoga—the fact that what our bodies learn as we become more in tune with the yoga practice emerges as part of our

"Though no one can go back and make a brand new start,
anyone can start from now and make a brand new ending."

—CARL BARD

everyday lifestyle. You'll see for yourself within the first few weeks. Here's what happens: As you discern what it feels like in your body to align with a posture, or to explore what it takes to hold a pose that requires balance, or to breathe into a new stretch, increasing your flexibility, you also begin to sense exactly what it feels in your mind to be aligned, balanced, and flexible.

Once you begin to practice yoga, you will discover that feelings or hunches about what you need to work on in your life start to become clearer. It is as if by clarifying what it means to be balanced, flexible, and strong in our bodies, we can now articulate these areas in our minds and therefore have more choice over bringing them more fully into our lives.

This will happen with focus and inner connection, as well. As you begin to focus on holding a particular pose, or as you concentrate on your breath, you not only learn about the posture, but you learn about the sensation of focus. You experience yourself as a person who is focused.

Let's face it, for many of us, our lives are so busy that if somebody told us to focus on one thing, we might not even know which one thing to start with. What yoga can teach us is that it isn't about which one to focus on—instead, it is about knowing what it feels like to be focused in the first place.

The same thing will be true as you learn about balance as part of your yoga practice. When you are developing a sense of balance in order to hold a yoga posture, you are learning what it feels like, inside, to be balanced. When your life is off-kilter, you now have a reference point within you; you now know what balance itself feels like, so you can bring that knowledge to your life. You can point at an area of your life and say, hey, I know what it's like to feel balanced, and this is not it. And then you have the choice to create more balance.

This is also key to reducing stress, as sometimes the most anxiety-producing factor in a situation is the fear that we have no control. Practicing yoga will not increase your ability to control the outcome of a situation, but as you learn to focus, stretch, relax, and balance, it can provide you with new choices in terms of how to respond in that

---

"Sitting quietly, doing nothing, spring comes, and the grass grows by itself."

—ZEN SAYING

> "Be observant if you would have a pure heart,
> for something is born to you in consequence of every action."
> —JELALUDDIN RUMI

situation. This gives you jurisdiction over how a stressful situation impacts you. The sense of empowerment and creative thinking that can result from realizing you have a choice over how to respond in a stressful situation—even though you cannot change the stressor itself—is one key to living a more healthy, loving, and fulfilling life.

And when you take the time to meditate after yoga, sitting with your energized, peaceful, powerful body and your quiet mind, you will discover who you are, inside, when you are aligned correctly. You will know what it feels like to be centered, to feel a flow of energy through you, and these will not just be concepts. They will be your experience.

This is exactly what allows you to make healthy choices in your life. When you know how good it feels to be solid, grounded, and powerful, then you can choose to make decisions that allow you to grow in that direction. Once you understand what it feels like to experience yourself as strong, focused, and balanced, then these are the choices you can make.

Finally, the greatest benefit of yoga is discovering the treasures within yourself that you bring to the practice. This is one reason why people who've been practicing for a while will tell you they feel fantastic. It's not just the firmer abs, the more flexible spine, and the luxurious flow of energy they're talking about. It's also the renewed perspective of one's self that taking the time to develop a practice can bring. It's making the priority to spend time enjoying what it feels like to come home to one's self, listening to what's going on inside. After all the studies are recorded and the mats are rolled up and stacked in the closet, it's the experience of honoring and celebrating your mind, spirit, and body that is the greatest reward of yoga.

✍   SUGGESTED READING   ✍

Benson, Herbert, and Proctor, William. *Beyond the Relaxation Response: How to Harness the Healing Power of Your Personal Beliefs.* New York: Times Books, 1994.

Benson, Herbert, and Klipper, Miriam Z. *The Relaxation Response.* New York: Avon, 1990.

Christensen, Alice. *The American Yoga Association Wellness Book.* New York: Kensington, 1996.

Dworkis, Sam. *Recovery Yoga: A Practical Guide for Chronically Ill, Injured, and Post-Operative People.* New York: Random House, 1997.

Francina, Suza. *The New Yoga for People Over 50: A Comprehensive Guide for Midlife and Older Beginners.* Deerfield Beach, Fla.: Health Communications, 1997.

Ornish, Dean. *Dr. Dean Ornish's Program for Reversing Heart Disease Without Drugs or Surgery.* New York: Ballantine, 1996.

Scaravelli, Vanda. *Awakening the Spine: The Stress-Free Yoga That Works with the Body to Restore Health, Vitality, and Energy.* San Francisco: HarperSan Francisco, 1995.

Schatz, Mary P. *Back Care Basics: A Doctor's Gentle Yoga Program for Back and Neck Pain Relief.* Berkeley, Ca.: Rodmell, 1992.

Shivapremananda, Swami. *Yoga for Stress Relief.* New York: Random House, 1998.

Stewart, Mary. *Yoga Over 50: The Way to Vitality, Health, and Energy in the Prime of Life.* New York: Simon & Schuster, 1994.

Whitelaw, Ginny. *Body Learning: How the Mind Learns from the Body: A Practical Approach.* New York: Berkley Publishing Group, 1998.

3.

The Different Schools of Yoga

As you read through the descriptions of the different schools in this chapter, remember that you do not have to choose one right now, although some beginners may want to get comfortable with one teacher and style before experimenting with a variety of approaches. For other students, spending a little time sampling different schools may be the best way to develop an individual practice. Keep in mind that many yoga teachers have studied in several schools, so while they may focus on a particular approach, they may also weave in teachings from a variety of styles.

When we talk about yoga's physical workout, we're actually only focusing on one branch of the practice: Hatha yoga. Hatha is one of the six branches of yoga. This branch focuses on the body and is the one most people are familiar with because it is the most commonly practiced. In a Hatha yoga class, students learn postures and breathing techniques that work together to develop balance, flexibility, strength, alignment, clarity of mind, and relaxation.

In the Sanskrit word *hatha,* *ha* is translated as "sun" and *tha* as "moon," which, when combined, describes the combining of complementary forces. The word comes to life in the practice, as postures are taught to evoke an integration of opposites. For example, when you learn a pose that contracts the body, you will also learn one that focuses on expansion.

"In each pose there should be a repose."

—B. K. S. IYENGAR

Hatha yoga was originally developed as a way to prepare for meditation. By practicing the postures, one could train the body and prepare the nervous system for the physical endurance and mental stamina required to still the mind. Today these postures are usually taught in part for meditation and in part for the physical and psychological benefits they offer.

The beginner can choose from a variety of approaches for learning the postures and breathing exercises of Hatha yoga, each of them unique. Some schools focus on the flow of breath as you move from pose to pose, and others concentrate on the posture itself, emphasizing accuracy and alignment in each position. Some schools use the movements of yoga to prepare for deep relaxation, while others offer breathing exercises to quickly awaken the mind and energize the nervous system.

A number of schools, or styles, exist within Hatha yoga.

When you are new to yoga, the array of schools can make you feel as dizzy as contemplating your first headstand, but it is useful to understand the different approaches that are available. This way, if your first class doesn't feel like it's really for you, you'll know it may be the style you need to reconsider rather than yoga itself. Getting a feel for the different schools will support you in having a positive experience as you begin your practice. For example, if you want a slow, relaxing way to end the day and you unknowingly register for an Ashtanga class (sometimes called power yoga), your yoga mat could end up in your next yard sale. A class based in Integral, Kripalu, or Viniyoga would better suit your needs.

Hatha yoga is the "yoga that we can feel, that we can experience, right here and right now. Hatha yoga is a powerful method for self-transformation. It is the most practical of all the yogas, and sages have recommended its practice in some form for millennia as preparation for all the other yogas."

—MARA CARRICO AND THE EDITORS OF *YOGA JOURNAL*, *YOGA JOURNAL'S YOGA BASICS*

> "The winds of grace blow all the time. All we need to do is set our sails."
> —RAMAKRISHNA

No matter which school of yoga you choose, one thing will remain the same: By starting a yoga practice, you will be experiencing your body in a new way. This is true whether you are a novice, whose exercise routine has consisted of walking between your house and your car; if you're a moderate fitness buff who jogs through the neighborhood three days a week, or even if you are training for a triathlon. For all beginning yoga students, in any school, at every level, the practice may activate unexpected feelings and thoughts. If you find yourself confused by what you are feeling, or surprised by some of the teachings—whether pleasantly or otherwise—feel free to share your thoughts. Most teachers will welcome any questions or concerns you have. Talking things over with the instructor, or with other students, will help you to further understand which school of yoga is best for your own needs.

Here's a brief description of nine different schools of yoga. You can contact the yoga centers listed at the end of this chapter to learn more about a particular school. Some centers will refer you to classes that are taught in your area. There are many other schools in addition to those listed here. Your teacher may describe his or her experience with a style that is not explored in this chapter. Every approach to studying Hatha yoga has its own unique value. What's important is to find the style—or styles—that suit your needs.

Viniyoga

Viniyoga is a slow, smooth approach to yoga. When compared to other schools, the aspect that makes it unique is its emphasis on individual needs and the flow of breath over the form and execution of the postures. In Viniyoga, postures are coordinated to move with the pace of breath. As you inhale and exhale, you may sink more deeply into a stretch, or discover that you can gently turn your spine just a smidgen more than you could on the previous exhalation.

Beginners who are looking for a relaxing, inclusive experience may feel comfortable in a Viniyoga class because of its slow pace, easy approach, and personal attention. The long, gradual stretches in Viniyoga offer an all-around workout and increase flexibility throughout the body, and the meditative, quiet pace directs the mind inward.

The founder of Viniyoga, Sri T. Krishnamacharaya, was a physician, healer, teacher, and astrologer. In addition to emphasizing the link between breath and movement, Krishnamacharaya believed in an approach to yoga that honors individual needs, interests, and capabilities. He developed techniques and principles to adapt yoga to different ages, physical conditions, and experiences.

"Viniyoga teachers are trained to read the bodies of their students and to adapt the class to what the student needs," explains Gary Kraftsow, who trains teachers and therapists in the Viniyoga lineage. "This means that a class can be slow or relaxing or highly energized. It all depends on the students' needs."

Krishnamacharaya died in 1989. His son, T. K. V. Desikachar, is one of the current holders of the lineage.

Ashtanga Yoga

Ashtanga yoga also synchronizes movements with breath, but it is in its own league in terms of physical exertion. Ashtanga is a high-energy, high-heat workout and is often practiced by athletes in search of a serious yoga routine.

"Yoga provides the means of bringing out the best in each individual. Doing this requires an understanding of a person's present condition or starting point, their potential, the goals that are appropriate for them, and the means available. Since each person is different, these will vary with each individual. The word Viniyoga suggests the ability to recognize these differences and to adapt the proper methods to each individual."

—T. K. V. DESIKACHAR

Ashtanga yoga has steadily increased in popularity over the past few years. It consists of practicing a challenging sequence of postures linked by the breath and taught in a room whose thermostat is turned up to match a summer afternoon in Miami. The speed and rigor of the practice—which includes a rapid sequence of postures—is designed to strengthen and stretch the body. The high heat helps to detoxify the body (through increased perspiration) and is believed to stoke the fires of the inner life force. The poses are designed to channel one's life force up the spine, leading to a feeling of meditative bliss.

Many newcomers to yoga will shy away from Ashtanga because of its reputation as an intense workout, but you might want to check out a class yourself before deciding. According to Beryl Bender Birch, author of *Power Yoga*, the level of difficulty can vary. "Some Ashtanga teachers are equipped to transition-in a be-

Ashtanga yoga is hard work, but those who hang in there with the practice praise it. Anne Cushman, senior editor of *Yoga Journal,* captured the love/hate relationship some students of Ashtanga yoga have when she described her own experiences. As a beginning student, you may relate to Cushman's reflections no matter what style of yoga you practice.

"In any given session . . . I gloat over poses I do well and rail against those I can't (most of which, I am convinced, are preposterous and shouldn't even be in the series in the first place)," she writes. "I shudder in revulsion as my neighbor, for the third time, exchanges his sweat-slimed mat for a fresh one. I nurse the delusion that if I could just hook both ankles behind my neck, the rest of my life would be nirvana.

"But then there are those moments that make it all worthwhile," Cushman continues. "I'm carried on my breath like a leaf in the wind: folding, arching, twisting, bending, leaping lightly from one posture to the next. My body tingles with energy; my mind is quietly absorbed in the hypnotic rhythm of the practice. The poses seem strung on the breath like prayer beads on a mala; I enter each one to the best of my ability, savoring the silky stretches, the pleasurable ache of muscles taxed to their edge.

"At moments like these," she believes, "I think I'm beginning to get a taste of what true Ashtanga practice might be like."

ginner more slowly and gently than others," she explains, "just like any other school of yoga.

"Beginners will learn about breathing and alignment right away with Ashtanga," she continues. "If that's what a new student is looking for, they should observe a class and then decide."

Ashtanga was developed by K. Pattabhi Jois, who teaches at his institute in Mysore, India, and is a disciple and lineage holder of Krishnamacharaya.

Iyengar Yoga

Have you ever visited a yoga studio and noticed a pile of canvas belts off to the side and a tower of wooden blocks in the corner? When classes are in session, these props help students of **Iyengar yoga** achieve and maintain postures.

The emphasis on posture is what makes the Iyengar school unique. That's where the props come in—they support both beginners and seasoned students to more fully explore the range of each pose. And though the image of belts and blocks may not conjure up feelings of a gentle, restorative practice, Iyengar is actually the most widely recognized Hatha technique in the Western world.

Its emphasis on posture teaches balance and alignment, and many students prefer to immerse themselves in attaining accuracy and precision in the different poses as a way to begin their yoga practice. In fact, some followers of Iyengar report that pursuing the exact alignment of each posture—instead of journeying from pose to pose as is practiced in some schools—is their favored method for calming the mind and experiencing strength, endurance, and improved energy.

Iyengar classes will include a reminder to watch the breath, but teachers pay more attention to the direction your knee points than to the way your exhalation flows between movements. A majority of the postures taught in an Iyengar class will be in standing positions, as these build strength and endurance and enhance one's awareness of placement. There is a great deal of personal attention in an Iyengar class, as the teacher usually roams between mats offering feedback to help students discover greater symmetry and extension in their postures.

As in any yoga class, Iyengar sessions balance an active pose with a brief restorative posture. With the use of props, however, the exploration of the restorative aspect of Iyengar yoga has developed into a focus all its own, called, most aptly, restorative yoga. It is a form of "active relaxation," designed for times when students feel fatigued or are bearing the experience of a major life change or illness.

The sequences taught in restorative yoga offer a flexibility tune-up for the spine, and the gentle breathing provides a soothing, nurturing journey inward. The inclusion of props—even something as simple as rolled blankets slipped under the knees when the student is on her back—helps to provide a supportive environment. According to Judith Lasater, author of *Relax and Renew: Restful Yoga for Stressful Times*, "By supporting the body with props, we alternately stimulate and relax the body to move toward balance."

B. K. S. Iyengar, the author of *Light on Yoga*, founded the school and is widely renowned for his development of therapeutic applications of Hatha yoga. He is considered by many to be a living master of Hatha yoga, and teaches at the Ramamani Iyengar Institute in Pune, India.

"You may be 50 years old, or 60 years old, and ask yourself whether it is too late in life to take up yoga practice. One part of the mind says, 'I want to go ahead,' and another part of the mind is hesitating. What is the part of the mind that is hesitating? Perhaps it is fear. What produces that fear? The mind is playing three tricks. One part wants to go ahead, one wants to hesitate and one creates fear. The same mind is causing all three states. The trunk is the same, but the tree has many branches. The mind is the same, but the contents of the mind are contradictory. And your memory also plays tricks, strongly reacting without giving a chance to your intelligence to think.

"Fear says that as you get older, diseases and suffering increase. Your mind says you should have done yoga earlier, or you should have continued and not stopped in your youth. Now you say you are very old and perhaps it is too late, so you hesitate. It is better just to start, and when you have started, maintain a regular rhythm of practice."

—B. K. S. IYENGAR

"You do not need to be doing great things. In your own small way,
among your neighbors, around your house, see that you are a friend to everyone.
Learn to love everyone equally, no matter what he or she is."
—SRI SWAMI SATCHIDANANDA

Integral Yoga

Beginners to yoga will find a combination of postures, breathing, and meditation in an **Integral yoga** class. Integral yoga was developed by Swami Satchidananda, whose opening talk at the Woodstock rock festival in 1969 included leading the sea of attendees in chanting "om."

Integral yoga classes are peaceful, and for the novice they provide a predictable routine—so even when the idea of yoga is new, the structure of each class is familiar. Sessions begin with forty-five minutes of postures, followed by deep relaxation, a breathing sequence, and a meditation. The postures are challenging, and teachers of Integral yoga are thorough and attentive in their instruction. The class is a quiet journey of stretching the body and calming the mind.

The focus on the breath in Integral yoga is similar to that of Viniyoga, as students learn to be mindful of how the flow of the breath aligns with the poses. The investigation of different postures is also woven through a class, as students are encouraged to discover what each pose offers in terms of stretch, release, and flexibility.

Swami Satchidananda, a student of Swami Sivananda, established the Integral Yoga Institute in 1966. It is now called Integral Yoga International and is headquartered in Yogaville, near Buckingham, Virginia.

Kundalini Yoga

The practice of **Kundalini yoga** is enlivening. Even beginners will feel a sense of awakening, as the breathing techniques used are designed to stimulate the nervous system and leave the mind feeling sharp and alive.

Kundalini yoga uses the breath, postures, and meditation to stimulate Kundalini energy, which is believed to be dormant at the base of the spine until aroused through yoga or other techniques. The result is a feeling of being both centered and a little bit "buzzy" at the same time, as breath work gets the energy moving quickly while the postures and meditation keep the body grounded and the mind focused.

Classes are supportive for beginners, who will most likely find a combination of great enthusiasm and gentle acceptance from a Kundalini teacher. The breathing methods may feel unusual to begin with, but once you become comfortable with each technique, its benefits are easily felt. For example, one method requires the student to rapidly alternate the breath between nostrils, which is accomplished in part by holding a finger against the side of the nose to keep one nostril closed. This is a simple gesture but can feel unfamiliar for beginners—though as soon as you get the knack, the rejuvenating sweep of energy and clarity of mind that it provides makes it worth getting beyond the hesitancy.

This school of Kundalini yoga was introduced to the West in 1969 by Yogi Bhajan. Many teachers and students of Kundalini are members of wider community called the Happy, Healthy, Holy Organization, or the 3HO, which focuses on a yogic lifestyle that includes a vegetarian diet, community service, and family values. 3HO sponsors retreats, yoga camps, and training, and beginning students are welcome to attend occasional potluck dinners or other community events.

Bikram Yoga

Where Kundalini yoga is known as 3HO, **Bikram yoga** could be called 2H: Heat and Hollywood. Bikram yoga, also known as "yoga to the stars," is practiced in a well-heated room and is popular with celebrities.

This is an action-oriented workout. Newcomers to yoga who are already engaged in a high-endurance fitness routine may find incredible pleasure and satisfaction in a Bikram yoga class. Novices are welcome, but should approach the class knowing what they are getting into. A Bikram yoga class consists of twenty-six postures, which include one-legged stances, backbends, twists, and other challenging positions, most of which are held for at least ten seconds. This approach gives you great muscle tone and strength. The classes open and close with breathing exercises designed to stoke internal heat, called **tapas.**

People are drawn to Bikram because the overall workout and extra attention given to building up heat create light, clean, and reenergized feelings throughout the whole body. Bikram differs from Ashtanga yoga in that there is more emphasis on holding the postures for a longer period of time, and the same twenty-six-posture sequence is followed each time in every Bikram class. Bikram classes also place a greater emphasis on building strength and balance in the legs by holding a series of one-legged standing postures in the first half of each class.

The style was developed by Bikram Choudhury, who opened his first school in Bombay, India, in 1965. He is now based in Beverly Hills.

Kripalu Yoga

Kripalu yoga is a choice that many newcomers make because it teaches the basic mechanics of yoga, introduces the concepts of breath work, and invites students to focus inward on the spiritual dimensions of the practice. The variety of postures taught

---

"Just as the purpose of Zen archery is not merely to hit the target, the purpose of the martial arts not just to overcome the enemy; and the purpose of koans not merely to find the answer to a question; so also in Kripalu Yoga, the purpose of the practice of asanas is not merely to perfect the posture or their physical benefits, but rather to use them as a tool to transcend the limitations of the ego mind, and to awaken to our highest potential."

—YOGI AMRIT DESAI

---

in a Kripalu class is challenging, but at the same time the coordination between movements and breath is relaxing. In fact, some beginners have described Kripalu yoga classes as an experience of "falling in love" with their bodies. Kripalu teachers emphasize the importance of accepting the body, encouraging students to note where tension is held or simply to recognize strengths and weaknesses.

Kripalu yoga is taught in three levels. Beginners learn a gentle method, briefly holding poses and gaining an awareness of how their bodies feel as they explore different postures. Students at the next stage learn to prolong the poses, exploring their own will as they maintain a position, and experiencing surrender as they breathe into the stretch. This stage also cultivates meditation, as students learn to focus inward in order to stay with the posture.

The third stage reflects the inspiration of the Kripalu founder, Yogi Amrit Desai. Yogi Desai developed Meditation in Motion, which is a deep listening to the wisdom of the body and a spontaneous flow of postures and movement. Students in this stage are encouraged to go with their impulses, enjoying the freedom of movement and the depth of inner discovery that this kind of open exploration offers. Some Kripalu-trained teachers offer a hybrid of this called DansKinetics, which progresses from gentle yoga exercises to rousing rock 'n roll and back to calming, integrative meditation within one session.

The Kripalu Center for Yoga and Health, a retreat center founded by Yogi Desai, is located in Lenox, Massachusetts. Its extensive training program has certified hundreds of Kripalu instructors over the last two decades.

Sivananda Yoga

Beginning yoga students are sometimes surprised by the plethora of books and materials available on the subject. Most bookstores carry a large number of titles, and even small yoga studios often fill a bookcase with texts, videos, cassettes, and CDs for students of all levels to borrow or buy.

This, of course, was not always the case. At one time, the most widely read book available was *The Complete Illustrated Book of Yoga*, written in 1960 by Swami Vishnu-devananda. Swami Vishnu-devananda, like Swami Satchidananda, the founder of Integral yoga, was a disciple of Swami Sivananda. The popularity of the book—still considered a classic—and the easily learned routines of the classes have made **Sivananda yoga** one of the world's largest schools of yoga.

Sivananda teachers weave a five-point philosophy throughout every class, so students are introduced to principles of relaxation, exercise, breathing, diet, and positive thinking in each session. Most classes follow a dependable sequence of breathing exercises, a routine of postures and deep relaxation. The classes open and close with a brief session of chanting and meditation.

Newcomers who are looking for a class in which they can become comfortable with a familiar series of poses and acquainted with yoga's affirming lifestyles and who want to offer their spiritual side a boost through meditation and chanting will find a supportive atmosphere in a Sivananda class.

Swami Vishnu-devananda founded the Sivananda Ashram Yoga Camp in Val Morin, Quebec, and the Yoga Retreat in the Bahamas, which has become a well-loved yoga get-away for students of all levels.

Ananda Yoga

Ananda yoga's distinction is its method of teaching specific affirmations, or positive thoughts, to accompany different poses. Every posture is viewed as an opportunity to expand one's self-awareness. Students are taught to incorporate statements that reflect the movement—for example, when lifting the heart and shoulders in the Cobra pose, the affirmation is "I rise joyfully to met each new opportunity."

For the beginner, an Ananda class offers an easy introduction to postures in an encouraging atmosphere. Students may find that some Ananda instructors spend as

> "Truth is no theory, no speculative system of philosophy,
> no intellectual insight. Truth is exact correspondence with reality.
> For man, truth is unshakable knowledge of his real nature, his Self as soul."
> —PARAMAHANSA YOGANANDA

much time on deep relaxation and meditation as on teaching different postures. The classes are gentle and evenly paced.

Ananda yoga was developed by J. Donald Walters, an American who followed the teachings of Paramahansa Yogananda, who was a pioneer in introducing Hatha yoga to America, author of *Autobiography of a Yogi,* and founder of the Self-Realization Fellowship. Yogananda taught yoga as a tool for cleaning and energizing the system in preparation for meditation. Walters founded the Ananda World Brotherhood Village, a residential community in Nevada City, California, in 1968.

Finding the Class That's Right for You

Now that you have a general idea of some of the different kinds of yoga you can choose from, here are some thoughts about how to make the right choice.

First of all, the beginner sees a lot of bodies during the search for the right yoga class, and they can be really interesting to watch. This is where your parents' advice to not worry "about what the other kids can do" will really come in handy, because choosing a class is a process of forgetting about everybody and recognizing your own needs and limitations. You will see other rookies, and you may wonder how they can stretch longer and twist farther and breathe more deeply than you can. Or you may make the happy observation that, in fact, you are the one who can stretch the farthest, and you just started. You might see old-timers who can stand on their heads with more tolerance than you have standing in a checkout line.

It's natural to compare yourself to others in the room, but don't dwell on it. They don't have to live with your body, you do. What may appear to be an impossible pose for one person might be a breeze for you, and vice versa. Take the time to reflect on your experience as you try each class. Make the choice that feels best for you.

It is also important to choose a teacher you feel comfortable with. In fact, though you might favor the description of a Viniyoga class, you may click with the Iyengar instructor—and that may be the best way to make your choice. Or you might admire the depth of knowledge one teacher has but prefer the personality of another, over and above the schools of yoga they are trained in. As you decide on a teacher, think about the learning style that feels most supportive to you. Do you like a hands-off

Tips for Finding a Teacher and Style That's Right for You

As you visit different yoga studios and experience a variety of teaching styles, here's a set of guidelines that will help you to decide on the right one for your needs:

✦ Remain aware of how your body feels. Have you been challenged at the physical level you are ready for?

✦ Be mindful of what you want to get out of the class. For example, are you feeling the sense of relaxation you were hoping for?

✦ Observe how you feel with the teacher. Talk to him or her about training and credentials, and get an idea of the kinds of things the class will emphasize.

✦ Let teachers know that you are looking around, and find out what other styles they might recommend.

✦ Listen to your words as you describe your experiences after class. Sometimes we tell ourselves one thing, but we tell our friends and loved ones another. Pay attention to how you talk about each class, because you may discover insights that can shed light on your search and your practice.

✦ Commit to a class once you find the right one. It is a commitment to yourself—keep going! You'll feel great.

approach, or do you want lots of individual attention? No matter which school a teacher is trained in, some will talk about yoga philosophy, others will discuss kinesiology and biomechanics, and others will simply lead the class through the poses. Give some careful thought to how the instructor's approach might influence your experience of yoga.

Once you find a teacher and school you feel confident with, you can expect to feel really good when you walk out of your yoga class. You will most likely discover a satisfying combination of serenity, energy, and focus, all at the same time. But there's a chance the first few classes may feel uncomfortable, as well. What's important to remember is that even the class that feels a little "off" might be the right one for you. Sometimes the different postures, or the moments of stillness, or just the creaks of a body that's more accustomed to an office chair than a yoga mat can be unsettling. This is normal.

If this is your initial experience, ask yourself what it is you want to get out of your yoga practice. Is it just to feel good? Or are you looking to push your edge a little bit, not just in terms of the body, but inside yourself, as well? Sometimes a class feels a little "off" because the feelings that began to surface during meditation were uncomfortable. Or the teacher went too quickly. Or he was plodding along, reviewing things you already knew, so you began to feel anxious.

These could be reasons to consider other classes, but more than likely, they will come up in the yoga studio around the block, as well. That's because a yoga class can be a magnified experience of the phrase "Wherever you go, there you are." At some point, no matter who teaches the class and what school they were trained in,

Remember to give your yoga class a serious try before deciding to switch to another. Think about looking for a class as if you were searching for water. In that case, you may be more successful when you find a likely spot and dig one well twenty feet than if you start ten different wells, each of them two feet beneath the surface.

you are the one on the mat, time after time. Therefore, what your yoga practice may be telling you is that the experience you are having could be originating inside you.

If you feel agitated because the teacher is painstakingly slow, here's your chance to take a look at impatience in your life. Or if you feel left in the dust after a quick round of Salutations to the Sun, take a look at why you feel such an urgency to keep up in the first place. Can't tolerate those final seconds of holding a pose? Do you choke up a little when you lift your arms wide above your head, exhale slowly, and open your heart? Ultimately, a yoga class should leave you serene and happy. But if you have these kinds of experiences, as well, they may not be reasons to try another class. In fact, they might be the best reasons to stay right where you are.

Finally, remember that the person up in the front of the room who can twist her spine like a rubber band was once a beginner just like you. In fact, every time your teacher moved from one level of yoga to the next, and then eventually into teacher training, he experienced what it was like to be a beginner, so he will empathize with how you are feeling. Talk to your teacher about the experience of the class—whether it is one of joy or confusion. When exploring different schools, check in with the teacher and other classmates. This can be a great help in deciding on which class to stay with.

YOGA CENTERS AND GROUPS

Ashtanga Yoga Center. 118 West E Street, Encinitas, CA 92024. (760) 632-7093.

Bikram's Yoga College of India. 8800 Wilshire Boulevard, 2nd floor, Beverly Hills, CA 90211. (310) 854-5800.

Center for Viniyoga Studies. PO Box 1662, Kahului, HI 96733. (808) 572-1414.

The Expanding Light (Ananda yoga). 14618 Tyler Foote Road, Nevada City, CA 95959. (800) 346-5350.

The Hard and the Soft (Astanga yoga). Beryl Bender and Thom Birch, 325 E. 41st Street, #203, New York, NY 10017-5916. (212) 661-2895.

Healthy, Happy, Holy Organization (Kundalini yoga). Route 2, Box 4, Shady Lane, Espanola, NM 87532. (505) 753-0423.

Jiva Mokti Yoga Center. 404 Lafayette Street, 3rd floor, New York, NY 10003. (212) 353-0214.

B. K. S. Iyengar Yoga National Association of the United States. 1-800-889-9642.

Kripalu Center for Yoga and Health. P.O. Box 793, West Street, Lenox, MA 01240. (800) 741-SELF.

Satchidananda Ashram-Yogaville (Integral yoga). Route 1, Box 1720, Buckingham, VA 23921. (800) 858-9642.

Sivananda Yoga Vedanta Center. 243 West 24th Street, New York, NY 10011. (212) 255-4560.

Yoga International's Guide to Yoga Teachers and Classes. Route 1, Box 407, Honesdale, PA 18431. (800) 821-YOGA.

SUGGESTED READING

Birch, Beryl Bender. *Power Yoga: The Total Strength and Flexibility Workout.* New York: Simon & Schuster, 1995.

Cushman, Anne, and Jones, Jerry. *From Here to Nirvana: The Yoga Journal Guide to Spiritual India.* New York: Riverhead Books, 1998.

Desikachar, T. K. V. *The Heart of Yoga: Developing a Personal Practice.* Rochester, Vt.: Inner Traditions, 1995.

Iyengar, B. K. S. *Light on Yoga.* New York: Schocken, 1995.

Iyengar, B. K. S. *The Tree of Yoga.* Boston: Shambhala, 1989.

Khalsa, Shakti P. K. *Kundalini Yoga: The Flow of Eternal Power.* New York: Perigee, 1998.

Kriyananda, Sri. *The Hindu Way of Awakening: Its Revelation, Its Symbols.* Nevada City, Ca.: Crystal Clarity, 1998.

Lasater, Judith. *Relax and Renew: Restful Yoga for Stressful Times.* Berkeley, Ca.: Rodmell, 1995.

Lidell, Lucy, and Rabinovitch, Narayani and Giris. *The Sivananda Companion to Yoga.* New York: Simon & Schuster, 1983.

Mehta, Silva, and Mihra, Shyam. *Yoga: The Iyengar Way.* New York: Knopf, 1990.

Satchidananda, Sri Swami. *Integral Yoga Hatha.* Buckingham, Va.: Integral Yoga, 1995.

Sivananda Yoga Vedanta Center. *Yoga Mind Body.* New York: DK Publishers, 1996.

Vishnu-devananda, Swami. *The Complete Illustrated Book of Yoga.* New York: Crown, 1995.

Taking Your Practice Off the Mat

4

Now that you have an understanding of the benefits of yoga and the different styles to choose from, let's take a closer look at how the study of yoga might create positive change not only in your body but emotionally and spiritually, as well.

This is where the meaning of yoga—to create union—is brought to life by unifying the mind, body, and spirit. The benefits of yoga are realized when each part is working together, allowing you to feel healthier and more at peace.

There's a phrase you may hear as you begin to take classes. "Your true yoga practice will start when you walk out of the classroom door," teachers and students might say. At first it may sound ironic, but as you become acquainted with your practice you'll probably find yourself saying it to newcomers.

There are a few ways in which yoga comes to life outside of the classroom—or, as you may also hear people say, "off the mat." One has to do with the fact that re-

"Synchronizing mind and body is not a concept or a random technique someone thought up for self-improvement. Rather, it is a basic principle of how to be a human being and how to use your sense perceptions, your mind and your body together."

—CHÖGYAM TRUNGPA RINPOCHE

juvenating the body has a positive impact on the mind and emotions. Let's face it: When your yoga class adds a bounce to your step, life is simply a more joyful place to be.

In addition, any way in which we change the way we move our bodies will influence our thoughts while toning our muscles. This is because the body and mind are connected, so what we teach our bodies is also absorbed by our minds. For example, becoming more flexible physically can invoke flexibility in one's general outlook. Or, when you discover the sense of balance and power as you learn to "take a stand" in a yoga pose, you can transfer this lesson to other areas of your life.

Another way that yoga comes to life outside the classroom is using techniques of awareness and concentration to focus in everyday life. In this way, yoga becomes more

Who Put the Should in Your Shoulders?

The way we speak can tell a lot about how we might hold certain feelings in our bodies. For instance, if you ever feel tension in your upper back, it could be one way of experiencing your inner voice when it tells you that you "*should* be doing such and such"—and expressing it through your *shoulders.*

Here are some other phrases used in everyday speech that reveal how feelings are experienced in the body:

+ Gut reaction

+ Pain in the neck

+ Broken heart

+ Open heart

+ Knee-jerk reaction

+ Can't stomach that

Can you think of more?

than the practice of postures. "Yoga means learning to pay attention," says Beryl Bender Birch. "If we find ourselves becoming more mindful as we brush our teeth, or work in the garden, or spend time with a friend, this is part of our yoga practice."

For some, this increased level of awareness is where the spiritual component of yoga comes in. By being in the present moment, one can feel a greater connection with the rest of the world. Here the yogic idea of union reflects a stronger link with all living things.

Beginners can rest assured that this is not a form of spirituality that has to do with a particular deity or doctrine. Learning to do yoga will not interfere with practicing your faith—in fact, it may enhance the connection you feel with God, or your higher power, in your prayers, fellowship, or performing service.

Erich Schiffmann, writing in *Yoga: The Spirit and Practice of Moving into Stillness*, describes how spirituality may emerge from yoga practice. "As you move into the depths of stillness, subtle and powerful changes will become apparent in your life. These will be both profound and entirely welcome," he explains.

"You will become familiar with the creative God Force inside you, the energy at your core. The world will look more beautiful because you're seeing it as it is, without the distorting influence of your conditioning," he continues. "You will feel different, happy for no apparent reason. It will seem as though you have undergone an important change, a rebirth, as though you've become a new person, and yet you will feel yourself more than ever before."

Yoga can also come to life outside the classroom by following the first two guidelines, or "limbs," of yoga. The eight limbs of yoga describe the comprehensive, life-affirming philosophy of the practice as outlined in the ancient Yoga Sutras of Patanjali.

Yoga is beneficial whether you know anything about its philosophy or not, but as a beginner, becoming familiar with the eight limbs of yoga is helpful because it offers a context in which to understand information that might be new to you. Even

---

"What matters is that for a time one be inwardly attentive."

—ANNE MORROW LINDBERGH

---

if your instructor never mentions the Sutras, simply by studying yoga one is touched by these teachings, as the eight limbs of yoga offer groundwork for moral and ethical conduct. They teach us that health and spirituality contribute to living with integrity. They encourage self-discipline and they enhance our ability to gain perspective on our lives.

For example, many novices will enjoy breathing techniques right away—most of them are simple to learn, they feel good, and when taught in a seated meditation position they provide a break from some of the more unusual poses. But when you bring an understanding of the way breath is described in the eightfold path as control of prana, or life energy, your perspective on breathing exercises is widened, which in turn deepens your experience.

The Limbs of Yoga

The first four of the eight limbs offer guidance on fine-tuning the areas we use in everyday life: our personalities and our bodies. These four limbs focus on self-discipline and physical awareness as tools that can help us develop into our fullest potential. They are beacons that light the way as we build our integrity, gain knowledge of our bodies, and begin to explore the possibilities of feeling more creative, healthy, and alive.

Yama

The first limb, Yama, is the granddaddy of the golden rule: "Do unto others as you would have others do unto you." This limb is actually made up of five **yamas,** each one an element of basic training for living a life of high standards, ethics, and in-

"It is not what you do that matters so much as why you do what you do. Motivation is the spirit of action. What you do is only the outer shell."

—YOGI AMRIT DESAI

tegrity. The function of a yama is to help you make life choices that are more true to your authentic, higher self. Living within these guidelines is also one way to help you to listen to—and to trust—the connection to your spiritual side.

The five yamas are:

Ahimsa: nonviolence or noninjury

Satya: truthfulness/nonlying

Asteya: nonstealing

Brachmacharya: continence, self-respect, and moderation of sense pleasures

Aparigraha: nongreed

Joan White, an Omega faculty member who has offered workshops in Iyengar yoga since 1984, uses the eight limbs to help beginners isolate and understand the subtleties of yoga. Using the second yama, truthfulness, for example, students may be asked to examine their integrity as they work to achieve a pose.

"If a student has to struggle to get into a pose, I ask them about how honest they are being with themselves. We look at the possibility of doing a partial pose instead. In this way, the yama teaches acceptance and awareness for the level the student is on, rather than pretending to be somewhere else."

Niyama

The second limb, niyama, provides five ground rules for self-discipline and inner work. Each one is a practice that supports spiritual observances—whether taking time for a peaceful walk alone or sharing fellowship with members of your church, temple, or meditation group.

The five **niyamas** are:

Saucha: purity, or inner and outer cleanliness

Santosha: contentment

Tapas: heat and austerity

Svadhyaya: self-study and scripture study

Isvara-pranidhana: surrender to a higher power

Asana

The third limb is called asana, which is the Sanskrit word used to describe the postures one learns in yoga. Every time you settle into a specific pose, you are developing the practice of asana. Because the body is the home of the spirit in yoga, being in touch physically strengthens the spirit and deepens self-discipline. Asana also helps prepare the mind for meditation.

Pranayama

Pranayama, the fourth limb, addresses mastering the respiratory process and understanding the links between breath, mind, and emotions. Yogis believe that pranayama not only rejuvenates the body but that its practice will prolong life itself. Pranayama can be integrated into a Hatha yoga routine or can be developed as an aspect of sitting meditation.

These first four limbs are designed to prepare the practitioner for the second four limbs of yoga, which assist in developing aspects of ourselves that most of us have less familiarity with: the senses, the mind, and a higher state of consciousness.

To a beginner, these may seem too advanced, but you may feel differently as you develop a practice. For example, the fifth limb, pratyahara, points to the process of gaining perspective on one's inner world. Though this is accomplished more successfully when the mind and body are trained to work in sync through the practice of the first four limbs, you may be ready to develop these kinds of insights as soon as you begin your practice. And for those who are new to yoga but have studied other forms of meditation, the seventh step, dhyana, may be more accessible.

Pratyahara

Pratyahara, the fifth limb, is the practice of drawing inside of oneself. This is the stage in which one trains the mind to shift awareness away from the external world, resting instead on what is going on within. This limb has a quality of detachment, as by practicing pratyahara we can step back and objectively observe the messages, habits, desires, criticisms, and dreams that inhabit our inner world.

Dharana

Dharana, the sixth limb, is the practice of concentration. Though the tools to develop concentration are available through asana and pranayama, this is the stage in which focusing is not a by-product of a posture or a breathing technique but is the practice itself. Here one trains the mind to slow down by focusing on a single mental object, such as an energetic point in the body, an image of a deity, or the silent repetition of a sound. The practice of dharana cultivates the mind for meditation.

Dhyana

Dhyana, the seventh of the eight limbs, is the stage in which one experiences stillness of the mind. It is distinct from the previous stage of concentration because it entails a state of becoming sharply aware but without focus.

Samadhi

This is where enlightenment comes in. The eighth limb has received a lot of press over the years, as it suggests the possibility of transcending the self and experiencing a feeling of divinity with all living things. Samadhi is the full realization of peace that many people yearn for.

The good news for beginners is that samadhi is an accessible experience. In fact, whispers and glances of it may be available every day. Some suggest that simply being present and savoring the "here and now" may offer a glimpse of enlightenment.

Taking It Off the Mat

In addition to the role that the philosophy of yoga may play in your life, just the fact that you are expanding your movement vocabulary and sharpening your awareness may initiate changes. Some of the ways in which yoga may show up in your everyday life are quite subtle—which reflects the innate beauty and wisdom of the practice.

A good illustration of this is in coordinating movement with breath, where even the gentlest of styles invoke the deeper teachings of yoga. For example, as you feel the ways in which your body responds when you relax into the flow of your breath, you may begin to gain insight into what you need to work on in order for other areas of your life to flow more smoothly. And because yoga teaches you to link movement with breath, you may begin to recognize when your actions are in sync with your intentions or to anticipate when you might unconsciously be working against yourself.

You may also have insights about how you identify boundaries in other areas of your life as you follow the breath from one pose to the next, quietly exploring the shape of the posture or recognizing the body's limits.

"Another reason the practice of asana, or yogic posture, can be a powerful transformational tool is its nonverbal nature. While practicing asana the student is using the right hemisphere of the brain, the one concerned with movement, the perception of the wholeness of patterns and spatial relationships, not words. Words generally divide thought, and it is this discriminative ability that gives words power. But that very ability to divide can divide us from ourselves, from our bodies and from our emotions. Because the asana is a nonverbal experience, there is not a filter of words between the student and the experience."

—JUDITH LASATER, PH.D.

Let's say you're in the Plough pose, with your legs extending out behind you, and you cannot get the tips of your toes to graze against the floor. You could try swatting your feet toward the floor, and then your toes would probably make contact. But that isn't practicing yoga, because in yoga the process of the movement takes precedence over the goal. Instead, you learn to tolerate the not-quite-there position. You learn to accept how far you are able to go.

Training the body to move with the flow of the breath can train the mind to flow more responsibly with the same kinds of not-quite-there situations off the mat. It's a lesson in patience, in flexibility, and in being in the present moment.

As the stretch progresses with your breath, eventually you may feel your toes tap against the floor. If so, you will have gotten this far by allowing your easy, long exhales to loosen the bend. In this case, you are also training yourself not to push when something isn't quite ready—a useful lesson to weave into everyday life.

Exploring alignment also offers insights that are applicable outside the studio. Even as a beginner, you can discover information about yourself just by checking out the placement of your body. When you stand relaxed, do your hips line up over your ankles, or are you leaning forward? If you discover a tendency to lean forward, you may also gain insight about a tendency to be "in the future" in your thoughts and actions. Now that you have this information, you might be able to catch yourself in a hurried moment and remind yourself, lovingly, to come back to the present.

In addition, as you learn to meditate, you will be training the mind to focus. You begin to learn what being present actually feels like in your body. You may not realize the strength of concentration you are developing, but there may come a day when

---

"I have a good friend, Rudolf Serkin, the pianist, a very sensitive man. I was talking to him one day backstage after a concert and I told him that I thought he had played particularly sensitively that day. I said, 'You know, many pianists are brilliant, they strike the keys so well, but somehow you are different.' 'Ah,' he said. 'I don't think you should ever strike a key. You should pull the keys with your fingers.'"

—ANDREW WYETH

---

you find yourself happily absorbed by an activity you would usually be distracted from. When you step back and think about it, you might recognize that the mindfulness skills you sharpened in the yoga studio are now coming into play at work, in a creative project, or as you listen to a loved one.

Even the simplest postures can offer us surprising insights into how the body and the lessons of expanding movement vocabulary relate to internal belief systems. Michael Lee, founder of Phoenix Rising Yoga Therapy, recalls experiencing this kind of "Eureka" when practicing the Standing Bow. "As we all know, taking a stand on anything requires courage, clarity, focus, commitment and self-expression," he says. "And for many of us, such qualities need to be strengthened. My yoga practice helped me to do this."

Lee recalls trying to do the Standing Bow—but doing more wobbling than standing—when his teacher asked, "Michael, how do you think you can stand on your own two feet when you can't even stand on one foot?"

"That didn't help my balance much," he remembers, "and I was also quite puzzled. Surely standing on one foot was more difficult than two, so what was he talking about? I clearly remember hating the posture as I tried in vain to regain my balance.

"Years later, while practicing the same posture," he continues, "a light went on: One of the secrets of all standing postures is where to put one's focus. I had discovered that if I could plant my focus firmly into my standing leg, visualizing it as a firm, strong, straight support, it would do its job and hold me in position while the rest of the posture happened above. That standing leg was my base, my rock of support."

This insight carried into the day-to-day for Lee. "We need to take care of our base (or our basics) before we can do much else," he explains. "We need to firmly direct our focus to our source of support, acknowledge it, feel it, enjoy it and then move out from it, trusting its ongoing presence. Otherwise, we are on shaky ground and will find ourselves without the platform needed for artful expression."

"When I marched with Martin Luther King in Selma, I felt my legs were praying."

—RABBI ABRAHAM HERSCHEL

This is when the words of his teacher came back to him. "I realized that strengthening each leg in turn gave me a different sense of myself while standing on two legs," he said. "By learning to support myself on one leg, it was so much easier to stand firmly on two, especially when focusing on them both.

"I also noticed inner shifts after making this connection," Lee continues. "I had more confidence, a greater capacity to take a stand in life with less fear of being knocked over, a greater willingness to face up to my challenges and the strength to endure whatever resulted."

The relationship among emotions, the body, and yoga is used to help people therapeutically in Phoenix Rising Yoga. Suzie Hurley, a yoga teacher and Phoenix Rising therapist, sees the relationship between body and mind in her classes and private practice every day. She advises beginners to be aware of the fact that feelings may emerge in their yoga practice that may be unexpected—ranging from joy to grief—but stresses that such feelings are a natural part of opening up the body.

For example, explains Hurley, beginners whose shoulders have rounded through years of sitting at a desk, or in response to emotions held in the body, may experience feelings around the heart area as they develop alignment. Standing with a straighter spine will open up the chest, perhaps releasing a sense of sadness. At the same time as a beginner's alignment improves, the lungs gain more space for breath, which gives the body a chance to be more invigorated and healthy.

"As the body opens," she explains, "there may be uncomfortable feelings that are not familiar, but this is one of the transforming aspects of yoga. As the body moves into more effective alignment, there will be a corresponding change. There may be a new willingness to let feelings in. At the same time, as beginners accept the emotions

---

"You have to go beyond words and conceptualized ideas and just get into
what you are, deeper and deeper. The first glimpse is not quite enough; you have to
examine the details without judging, without using words and concepts.
Opening to oneself fully is opening to the world."

—CHOGYAM TRUNGPA

---

and sensations that are part of them, without judgment, they may begin to experience life more deeply—which in turn means they can enjoy life more fully. And isn't this what practicing yoga—on or off the mat—is all about?"

Beginners will discover that though the teachings of yoga appear to be focused on the body, they actually permeate the whole life. It becomes easier to navigate through a busy schedule when the body is energized and the mind is clear. The person feels good, looks good, and greets the world with a renewed sense of confidence—which in turn inspires positive feedback. Bringing the lessons of yoga off the mat and into everyday life is a way of cultivating the innate joys that are available to us in even our most routine habits and ordinary interactions.

The most poignant ways in which the practice of yoga can embrace life is through increased awareness and acceptance. Awareness is about being in the moment, present to what is going on in the here and now. When we develop awareness, we start to understand how the choices we make affect our lives. We become aware of how we feel, inside, when our choices are healthy, creative, and life-affirming, and it is difficult to deny our feelings when things are not going well.

Once we gain this understanding, we may want to take a second look at some of our choices. We may want to make a change. If so, accepting ourselves is the first step, as we can change only what we accept. When yoga teaches awareness and acceptance, the practice offers us keys to personal responsibility. And this is the doorway to deep, meaningful change.

The true purpose of yoga is to unify—to yoke or join our small selves with the Infinite, the Supreme Universal Energy that courses through all living things, including ourselves. We then no longer feel separate from the things outside us nor within us, but directly experience the Truth and Oneness in all things. The six As are a way to help you move toward the true meaning of yoga.

The Three A's of Yoga

Yogi Amrit Desai taught students of Kripalu yoga about the "Three As"—awareness, acceptance, and adjustment. Acceptance is crucial, he taught, as you can't get to your destination if you don't know (and accept) where you are starting from.

"If you call a friend in California and say you want to go there, your friend needs to know where you'll be driving from in order to help you plan your route," he told his students. "The trip will be much different if you are leaving from Portland than if you are starting out in Canada."

The point is that being aware of where you are, and accepting it—physically, emotionally, and spiritually—is what allows you to lay out the map and chart the course of where you want to go. If you wish you were starting your drive to California from Portland, but you can look out your window and see the lights of Vancouver, you need to accept that the trip will be longer than you wanted it to be.

Once you accept the place where the journey is beginning, you can make the kinds of adjustments that support a successful trip. You can plan enough time, buy enough gas, and toss a variety of CDs into your duffel bag.

In the same way, if we want to change some of the circumstances or situations in our lives, we need to accept the choices, beliefs, and behaviors that define where we are now in order to understand how to reach our goal. Then we need to make adjustments—and this may require a heightened attitude of self-compassion. "The keys to the stage of adjustment are patience and moderation," according to the Kripalu Yoga Fellowship *Self-Health Guide*. "Often, we either want to go too far or too fast and become discouraged when we can't change everything overnight, or else we feel that the changes needed are so great we'll never be able to do it, so we are discouraged from even starting. The Kripalu Approach recommends gentle, gradual, easy-to-accomplish changes, starting with something we know we will find pleasant and not difficult. Then, encouraged by our early success, we'll feel inspired to continue into slightly more difficult areas without becoming discouraged. In other words, the whole process is a game we play with the subconscious mind, tricking it into giving up its grip on our old, nonproductive habits."

Suzie Hurley, who has trained at the Kripalu Center and now offers workshops there, teaches an expanded version of the Three As to her yoga students at the Willow Street Yoga Center in Takoma Park, Maryland. The three additional As were taught to Hurley by John Friend, a nationally renowned yoga instructor, and they work with the insights of the original three to help us to remember what yoga is about for our practice on the mat as well as in our lives. Hurley explains the Six As as follows:

AWARENESS

Awareness means being present —which means placing myself on the mat in my practice (or in my life situation) with focused intention and openness to what is in the moment. Without awareness, our minds are somewhere else and we are not doing yoga, whether on or off the mat. If we get lost trying to find a new place, there is no hope until we are aware we are lost!

We give ourselves a great gift in simply being present to what is. That includes our bad moods, aches and pains in the body, and all the other ten thousand things we'd rather not be present and aware of. It also includes being present to contentment, satisfaction, and joy that can be so abundant in our lives.

ACCEPTANCE

Now that I am in awareness, I find it both helpful and necessary to accept the strengths and limitations of my body-mind on that particular day.

I think too often that it is very easy to skip this important step. In fact, before transformation can take place, we must accept where we are. This is about finding the balance between pride and humility. We honor our strengths and our efforts, yet we know on some level that we are not the do-er, and also accept gracefully our limitations and weaknesses.

Acceptance brings us closer to a place of opening to that Grace. It is about creating a deeper acceptance that we are indeed a reflection of that Divine spark and worthy of recognizing our True Nature.

ADJUSTMENT

We can explore adjustment with micromovements, breath, feeling, and, most important, our very consciousness. In doing so we make whatever adjustments may help the pose itself. In the end, when energy is free to radiate out equally through every part of the body-mind, our spirit is contacted, nourished and expressed. The pose and the do-er become one.

Within adjustment are alignment, attitude, and action.

ALIGNMENT

Once we become aware of where we are, come to accept it, and begin to make adjustments, we can begin to think about alignment. How do we want to align our bodies so our energy may be most freely expressed, so there is both purposeful and focused effort, yet a nonstriving and nonclinging mind? This is not an easy task by any means.

Here is where we, in open exploration of the principles of biomechanical alignment, get to feel how the muscles, joints, and bones respond to ways of being in the pose. We get to feel what happens when we collapse in our lower backs, or when the hamstrings are pulled too tightly, or the thigh is not lifted, or when the breath stops.

When we can align our pose, both from a physical and an energetic perspective, energy is free to flow and a lightness, both in the body and of the heart, naturally comes into play. The tight, dark, tense places in our body-minds have an opportunity to loosen their grip as they are brought to light.

ATTITUDE

Now that we are present, we may choose the attitude we want for our practice. After all, the attitude we bring to whatever we do is the foundation for that particular endeavor's success or failure, and this is especially true in yoga. Our attitude is the source of expression of the pose, and therefore the pose will reflect when the attitude is tired, listless, restless, angry, ego-driven, or lazy. It is the most powerful and important factor in terms of inner transformation.

The attitude that usually works for me is what I call Opening to Grace, though I may also choose to bring a very energetic attitude to my practice, or conversely, an attitude of deep relaxation and breath to every pose.

ACTION

Action is expressed from the center of the pose in all directions. Our own personal expression of the posture comes to life with a feeling of expansiveness, lightness, and celebration. The same is true with action in our own lives—when we are aware of where we want to go and have accepted where we are before we make our plans to get there, our actions are centered, affirming, and energized with a sense of inner-knowing and purpose.

SUGGESTED READING

Christensen, Alice. *Yoga of the Heart: Ten Ethical Principles for Gaining Limitless Growth, Confidence, and Achievement.* New York: Daybreak Books, 1998.

Hendricks, Gay, and Kathlyn. *At the Speed of Life: A New Approach to Personal Change Through Body-Centered Therapy.* New York: Bantam, 1994.

Schiffmann, Erich. *Yoga: The Spirit and Practice of Moving into Stillness.* New York: Pocket Books, 1996.

Sturgess, Stephen. *The Yoga Book: A Practical Guide to Self-Realization.* Rockport, Mass.: Element, 1997.

Whitelaw, Ginny. *Body Learning: How the Mind Learns from the Body: A Practical Approach.* New York: Perigee, 1998.

The Self-Health Guide: a personal program for holistic living. Lenox, Mass.: Kripalu Publications, 1980.

5.

Working with the Breath

For many beginners, working with the breath is like uncovering a hidden treasure. This is ironic, of course, as the first thing every one of us does (it's hoped) when we enter this world is take a deep breath. Its life-critical importance never changes; we can skip a few meals, and we can tolerate thirst, but we cannot live without oxygen. But unless we are in the throes of a stuffy head cold, or a more serious respiratory illness, most of us take breathing for granted. By practicing yoga, we are offered the chance to explore breath more deeply, celebrating the vital connections among breath, spirit, energy, and health.

Though we need oxygen to survive, breath has more significance than simply the bringing in and letting out of air. In yoga, the breath is used to energize and cleanse the body. When one breathes properly, creating a complete change of air in the lungs, the oxygen level in the body increases, and that produces energy. With full, complete exhalations, the body rids itself of stale air, so there is plenty of space for all the new, fresh air to come in with the next inhalation.

"When one leaf trembles, the whole bough moves."
—CHINESE PROVERB

Breathing properly off the mat will improve circulation, increase concentration, and enhance energy. By controlling your breath, yogis believe, you can calm and relax your body.

Optimally, breathing should be full and rhythmic, and the diaphragm and ribs should be used to fill and empty the lungs. Unfortunately, many people do not do this. Poor posture, restrictive clothing, and a hurried life all interfere with breathing. This creates an unhealthy cycle, because the lack of sufficient oxygen brings on feelings of lethargy and fatigue. Once you begin to recognize the way you breathe, you have the choice to shift it at any time. The ability to reduce stress, awaken energy, and sharpen your focus is always available. Since you have to breathe anyway, why not make the most of it?

Breathing Tips

These tips are helpful in any of the breathing exercises described later in this chapter. They also come in handy when you need a quiet stress-buster. The next time you find yourself put "on hold" during a phone call, for example, check your breath. Is it on hold, as well? Or, when you are on your way to an important appointment and the freeway is locked in a snarl of cars, watch your breath. Does it stop and start according to the flow of traffic?

If so, try the following breathing tips. You may find that it is a better use of your time than feeling the frustrations that often emerge in these situations. In fact, you may complete the call or arrive at your meeting feeling relaxed and centered.

- ✦ Breathe with the abdomen. Allow your belly to expand as you inhale, both to the front and to the sides. Don't be shy—make a big belly. As you exhale, bring your naval toward your spine by contracting your lower abdominal muscles. This not only helps complete the exhalation but strengthens the area, as well.

- ✦ Keep your breathing long and even, and use your awareness to make sure the length of the inhalation matches that of the exhalation, and vice versa. Bring your attention to spending the same care and mindfulness with both.

- Breathe in and out through the nose. Doing so may not be what you are used to, but it may soon feel like the most comfortable way to breathe.

- Breathe with imagination. Whether you are in a posture, eyes closed, or are using a breathing technique to bring yourself back to center in the middle of that traffic jam—and thus have your eyes wide open—visualize the lengthening of your spine and opening of your chest with each inhalation. Work with the positive energy that is inside you. As you inhale, imagine light moving down your spine and up your center, bringing a gentle sense of warmth across your back and belly. As you let your breath out, ground yourself by directing your energy down, toward the earth. This not only helps you connect to your center but can tone the abdominal muscles, as well.

- Take the real pause that refreshes. Once you feel familiar with the preceding steps, and you feel the natural, easy rhythm of breathing from the belly, using equal breaths, try to pause consciously after each inhalation and exhalation.

It is important to maintain a sense of balance by pausing at the end of both the inhalation and the exhalation. Pausing at the end of each inhalation, called breath retention, helps to bring a feeling of expansion, heat, and energy to the body. Pausing at the end of each exhalation is known as suspension, and it activates the more pacifying qualities of coolness and relaxation. Keep each pause to about five seconds.

Taking this brief moment to pause is a way of savoring the delicious feeling of relaxation that accompanies mindful breathing. If your life is one of zipping from one thing to the next, however, the act of pausing to feel something—even something as simple as the breath—might feel like an imposition. Even though it literally needs only a few seconds of your time, it can still become one more thing you have to do.

If you find yourself having these thoughts, you are not alone. It is perfectly natural to resist the kinds of breathing tips discussed here. If that happens, appreciate yourself for your awareness—simply recognizing your hesitancy is a big step—and see if you can try them anyway. Remember, there is no hurry. Like taking steps, proper breathing begins one inhalation at a time.

"Your breathing is the key. Breathing brings the poses to life. It's what animates the stretches and gives yoga its fluidity and flow. As you immerse yourself in the flowing rise-and-fall rhythm of your breathing, you'll begin to sense that there really is only one breath, even an hour of yoga is just one long continuous stream of breath flowing in and out. The idea, the training, is to make your awareness as continuous as the breath . . . pay attention to your breathing; listen to it, feel it, taste it, savor and enjoy it."

—ERIC SCHIFFMANN

Breathing Exercises

These exercises are designed to be done by themselves or as a way of leading into your yoga practice. In addition to introducing you to using breath to still the mind, they will condition the muscles involved in the respiratory process.

In order to get the most from these exercises, put some thought into the space, time, and feelings you can make available.

Space

In terms of space, since some of the exercises are done lying down, make sure you have a broad, clean area on the floor. Make yourself comfortable by lying down on a rug, a yoga mat, or a folded blanket. Set up the space so it is free of distractions. You may need to turn the heat up a little and close the door to keep the cat from padding in and nuzzling your toes. Turn the lights down low.

Time

Use these breathing exercises as a way of giving yourself time alone. Make sure your household can operate without you, even for a few minutes. If your family is home, appoint another adult the kids can turn to, or for single parents ask the kids to give you ten minutes of quiet time. You might locate the little ringer button on your phone and switch it to "off." Decide on how much time you want to spend on the exercises, and then consider adding ten minutes.

The Meaning of Breath and Pranayama

The power of breath, with all of its meaning, is revealed through the roots of several commonly used English words. In this case, Daniel Webster can help "take it off the mat." For example, a derivative of *spirare,* which is the Latin root for respire, inspire, aspire, and expire, is *spiritus,* which means "the breath of a god."

If you open up your dictionary to "aspire," the Latin reads as "ad + spirare," or, "to breathe." We use the word, however, not just to describe breathing, but when we have high ambitions or desires.

In the same vein, leafing forward in the dictionary to "expire," we discover "ex + spirare," or to run out of breath. In its everyday usage, the word is applied to more than just breath, as anything that ends is said to expire—from magazine subscriptions to life itself. The importance of breath over and above its physiological function is clear here, as it illustrates the idea that any ending is linked to taking the last breath.

The final example, found just a few pages farther along in the dictionary, is even more revealing. The word "inspire," or "in + spirare," which we use when creativity is coursing through our veins or we are headed toward our wildest dreams, is literally defined as "adding breath."

Taking a similar look at the Sanskrit word used for "breath control" can heighten our experience of even the simplest breathing techniques. The word is *pranayama,* and, as a beginner, you will hear it often in your yoga classes. However, just as the meaning of a word such as "inspire" has another meaning than to simply "add breath," so pranayama is more than the act of controlling one's breathing.

Writing in the book *Yoga for Body, Breath and Mind,* A. G. Mohan says, "The meaning of the word pranayama can be confusing. It is often mistakenly thought to be composed of *prana* and *yama* (control) and is thus understood to mean 'control of the breath.'

"However," Mohan explains—and beginners to yoga and Sanskrit may want to take in a breath here—"pranayama is to be understood as *prana* and *ayama* (to lengthen, stretch, extend). Prana is a concept that means 'life force.' The prefix *pra* means 'very well' and *an* means 'to go' or 'to travel.'

"Prana, then," he continues, "is that which travels well through all parts of the body, inside us. It is the total energy that makes up a human being . . . prana exists in all living things."

Yoga works with what we have inside us, with what we bring to the mat. This is also true for prana. "We cannot acquire more prana from outside—by breathing into our bodies, for instance, " Mohan writes. "Rather, it resides within us and, when allowed to flow correctly, results in ideal functioning."

If pranayama is not the control of breath, then what is its relationship to our breath? Why is it the word associated with breathing exercises? "Breath is the expression of prana," Mohan explains, "the expression of life and the force behind it. While prana cannot be seen, touched, or directly manipulated, the breath is sort of a lever, or method, for working on it indirectly.

"When the breath is affected, prana is also affected . . . if yoga is a tool of reflection, pranayama may be seen as a means of sharpening this tool."

Posture

When you practice these techniques in a sitting posture, choose a straight-backed chair—comfortable but not cushiony. Keep your feet planted on the floor in front of you, hands resting on thighs or in your lap. If you are seated on the floor, you can choose to sit in lotus position or you can tuck your calves and feet under you. In all cases, keep your spine straight and your belly relaxed. Bring your attention to your shoulders, as well—are they slumping? If so, you can lift them and open up your chest by bringing your shoulder blades just a little bit closer. Move them gently when you do. Or are your shoulders pulled back, as if you're standing at attention? Right now you just need to *be* at attention. Let your shoulders fall if they are tense.

Feelings

Now check out how you feel. Wear comfortable clothing. Some people prefer leotards while others find that a big T-shirt and roomy pants feel cozy. Whatever you choose, make sure it fits around your waist in a way that gives you plenty of space to breathe.

The breath is intricately related to emotions, the nervous system, and the psychological state of being. If you are harboring pent-up feelings, they may surface during these exercises. If you feel in touch with your confidence and power, this may be heightened through the exercises. Whatever feelings come up, use the breath to sense them, then to let them go. Now simply relax, settle into the experience, and enjoy.

Exercise 1

Watching Your Breath

This exercise will help you to become familiar with your natural breathing pattern. It is done lying in a supine position on the floor. When you lie down, take a moment to allow your weight to sink into the floor. Raise your knees—keeping your feet flat on the floor—to help your lower back relax. Feel the blanket or mat where it touches your skin. Let your eyes gently close, and bring your attention to your natural breathing process. What moves in your body when you breathe? (Don't change anything at this point, as this time is reserved just to observe.) Do your chest and shoulders move? Does your belly rise? Scan your body with your mind, looking for areas of tension, or holding, especially in your face, shoulders, and neck. Are you breathing through your nose or mouth? Is the inhalation as long as the exhalation, and vice versa? Again, this is not a time to judge yourself but just to understand the nature of your regular breathing pattern.

Once you have established what your routine breathing pattern is like, you will be ready to move on to the next exercises. In this way, the idea of becoming aware and accepting "what is" before introducing change is integrated into breathing exercises.

The following exercises will guide you through an exploration of discovery about breath.

Exercise 2

Belly Breathing or Abdominal Breath

Again, lie down in a supine position with your knees raised, feet flat on the floor. Keep your eyes open, your gaze soft. Place your hands over your belly, bringing your attention to the abdomen.

Pause for a moment and think about your belly. This is an area of the body that many people have received negative messages about or have mixed feelings toward. Do you have a habit of trying to hold it in whenever you pass a mirror? Do you wish it were flatter, trimmer, or sexier? Some cultures believe the seat of power is in the belly, just below the navel. In today's world, people are subjected to a marketing culture that celebrates a waist size most adults haven't seen since the sixth grade. These messages can seep into our internal thoughts, creating tension in the belly that we are not aware of.

As you begin this exercise, feel the shape of your belly under your palms. Think about all the wonderful things it does for you—even if you are someone who has ambivalent feelings about what it looks like. Think about the gift of digestion your belly provides, which means you can be properly nourished. Consider the idea that this belly just might be your seat of power.

Now begin the breathing exercise. As you inhale, expand the abdomen into a round shape, allowing the breath to gently push it up against your hands, expanding from the center of your pelvis. Imagine your breath filling the sides of your body and expanding into your lower back.

As you exhale, totally empty the lungs. Softly press the belly down with your hands, making it concave or flat.

Practice this repetition about five times. The pace of this exercise begins slowly, with even, controlled breathing. Try a count of five to bring the breath in, then follow that with five to let it out. As you get comfortable you might try lengthening each breath, introducing a slight pause at the end of every one. As you exhale, let go of any

The Mechanics of Breathing

What's going on in there? As you practice your breathing, you may begin to feel new parts of your body. Here's what's actually involved in the mechanics of breathing.

The torso can be divided into three regions: the thorax, the abdomen, and the pelvis. The thorax, or chest, houses the heart and two lungs, and the abdomen, which begins immediately below the thorax, is separated from it by a sheet of muscle, called the diaphragm. The abdomen also contains the organs of digestion. Finally we come to the pelvis, which extends from the hipbones down to the bottom of the torso, housing the organs of excretion and reproduction. In terms of breathing, the pelvis is considered to be continuous with the abdomen.

The torso can be viewed as forming a rough cylinder. An increase in its volume, and consequently its inhalation, can be produced by one of three means: extending the diaphragmatic floor of the cylinder downward, expanding the walls outward, or moving the top of the cylinder upward.

THREE PHASES OF BREATHING

These three ways of expanding the torso are called diaphragmatic, thoracic (or chest), and clavicular.

Diaphragmatic breathing is physiologically the most efficient. A major portion of the blood circulating in the lungs goes to the lower portions or gravity-dependent parts, and expansion occurs in these lower portions. It is interesting to note that infants and small children use their diaphragm exclusively.

A second major way of breathing is to expand the diameter of the thorax—or the chest—which involves expanding out, so you are actually moving the ribs around their joints of attachment to the vertebrae. Chest breathing fills the middle and upper portion of the lungs with air but is not as efficient with the lower portion.

The third type of inhalation, clavicular, is significant only when the maximum amount of air is needed. Its name derives from the clavicles, or collarbones, which are pulled up slightly at the end of the maximum inhalation. This expands and lengthens the top of the thoracic cylinder and thus the very top of the lungs.

PUTTING THEM ALL TOGETHER

The three types of inhalation can be coordinated into one smooth exercise. This is the yogic complete breath, and it has a diaphragmatic, thoracic, and clavicular phase. Each phase of inhalation acts in sequence in one particular area of the lungs. When a rasping sound is added to this, it becomes the ujjayi breath.

+ First, the breath is initiated by diaphragmatic contraction, resulting in a slight expansion of the lower ribs and protrusion of the upper abdomen, thus oxygenating the lower lung fields.
+ Second, the middle portions of the lungs expand, with outward chest movement as inhalation proceeds further.
+ Third, additional air is drawn in by slightly raising the clavicles, thereby expanding the uppermost tips of the lungs.

tension, paying particular attention to anyplace that may have felt tense in the first breathing exercise.

This is the most important of the breathing awareness techniques. Deep, abdominal breathing lends a calming effect to the whole system and massages internal organs. The movement of expansion and contraction works to tone the musculature of this area, as well. This not only strengthens the abdomen but can leave you feeling grounded and solid and increases the awareness of your center. This will become evident as you work with postures that require balance.

Exercise 3

Chest Breathing—Intercostal Breath
or Athlete's Breath

This exercise is similar to belly breathing but shifts the focus to the chest area. The pace of the breath remains the same, with equal time spent on the inhalation and exhalation. Again, count to five or so, and try to lengthen the breath as you go deeper into the exercise.

> "The greatest thing in the world is for a man to know how to be himself."
> —MONTAIGNE

Place your left hand on your chest area—over your heart, which is under the sternum, between the breasts—and the right hand on your lower abdomen. As you inhale, fill your longer lungs, which will expand the belly but also direct the breath up into the chest area. Try to expand your rib cage. The movement here will be subtler than it was with the belly, but you will still feel your hand rise.

Again, just as with the belly breathing exercise, take a moment to think about this part of your body. The heart is considered to be the seat of emotions. We all know these familiar phrases: "heartbroken," "brave heart," "heartfelt." Allow yourself to get a sense of the joys and sadness that have visited your own heart. Acknowledge that through it all, your heart keeps on beating, doing a miraculous job of pumping fresh, healthy blood through your system.

Imagine, with each inhalation, that positive, life-affirming energy is being drawn in and nourishing your heart. With each exhalation, let go of any "heartache" that keeps you from the abundance and love that is your "heart's desire."

This technique can be more stimulating than belly breathing because of the additional emphasis placed on the chest and the sense of freedom and peace the visualization may offer.

The first three breathing exercises will enhance your awareness of breathing, tone your respiratory muscles, and begin to awaken the connection among breath, emotions, and the body. The next five move beyond the goal of developing awareness and into classic pranayama repertoire. They are unique methods of breathing utilized to evoke specific responses. They can be practiced in seated or kneeling positions, or coordinated with the movements of yoga postures.

Exercise 4

Victorious Breath—Ujjayi

The literal meaning of the term *ujjayi* means "she who is victorious." Other connotations reflect superiority in rank, success and triumph, and imply restraint or curbing. Some say that this ujjayi helps in recalling and working with dreams.

This breathing technique is connected to sound, and once you get the hang of it, it may sound like the *Star Wars* character Darth Vader. You can also think about breathing out as if you are trying to fog a mirror. Here's how it works.

First, imagine that your throat is the size of a straw and, like a straw, can be used for both drawing up and directing out. Now, as you breathe in through the nose, create a low, sibilant sound by slightly contracting the throat as you draw the breath down the back of the throat. In other words, imagine drinking in the air with your throat. When you exhale, feel the breath at the back of the throat, as if it is being pushed out a small tube.

Ujjayi is helpful on many levels, especially for newcomers. It is best to practice it for a few minutes in the beginning and then incorporate it into your postures. Listening to the sound can offer insight into your well-being. A smooth, even sound suggests a calm constitution, while a rough, choppy one may indicate agitation or imbalance.

The practice of ujjayi helps to increase the amount of oxygen that is drawn into the lungs, which enhances the respiratory system. The technique also reduces phlegm and strengthens the immune system. When combined with movement, its steady pace and focus on sound create an all-around, satisfying workout. Beginners who weave ujjayi into their practice may discover that it accelerates the experience of a unified body and mind, leaving them calm, rejuvenated, and connected to a deeper, more sacred part of themselves.

Exercise 5

Bee Breath—Bhramari

This technique also uses sound, but this time you'll sound like a bee. The word translates to mean "she who roams," as a bee roams.

In a seated position, take a deep inhalation, filling your lungs. Squeeze in just a little more air than you thought you could. Now, as you exhale very slowly out of the nostrils, make an "mmm" sound, much like the buzz of a bee. This will create a slight vibration. Direct the vibration to the facial area between the tops of the teeth and the eyes.

As the sound disappears with the end of the exhalation, contract your ribs and compress the area a few inches above the navel to fully expel the air.

Repeat this five times, taking all the time you need to float along the sound fully. This technique vibrates and opens the sinuses, clears the mind, calms the nerves, and helps to tone the abdominal muscles.

Exercise 6

Om Breath

This is a breathing method that uses a **mantra,** which is a sound that creates a feeling of peace and unity when it is said in a chant or as part of meditation. In this case the sound is "om."

There is an ancient yogic belief that if all of life were translated into a single sound, that sound would be "om." Though there is no way of testing this, there is lots of evidence that many people who use this breathing technique find that it clears the mind and leaves them feeling balanced and calm.

Ten thousand flowers in spring, the moon in autumn,
A cool breeze in summer, snow in winter.
If your mind isn't clouded by unnecessary things,
This is the best season of your life.

—WU-MEN

You can practice the om breath whether you are standing, sitting, or lying down. It is often done in groups because of the deep feeling of unity that chanting the sound together can create. To do the om breath, simply take a deep breath and sing out the "O" sound with a steady voice. This is an opportunity to hear the strength of your own voice, so feel free to allow your throat to open and the sound to grow. As the "O" sound comes to a close, gently close your lips and let the "MMMMM" sound follow. It should feel like a vibrating hum.

Once you have finished the sound of your first om, take a deep breath and try it again. Notice how the sound and vibration keep you focused on your breath and keep your mind from wandering. Repeat five times.

Exercise 7

C o o l i n g   B r e a t h :   S i t a l i

This is an unusual technique, included here as an interesting variation on regular abdominal breathing. Sitali is great for summer, as it cools the body. This technique employs the idea of using a straw again, but this time the straw is used for the tongue, not the throat. And, this time, it's more than just an image.

To do sitali, roll the tongue into a tube and let the tip of it peek just a little bit outside the mouth, resting on your lips. If you are not genetically disposed to rolling your tongue, just let it rest on your lips.

Now, draw the breath in through the curled tongue, filling your lungs. Once the lungs are full, bring the tongue back into your mouth, and close the mouth. Lower your chin, retaining the inhalation for a few seconds, and let the exhalation out through the nose. Begin again by inhaling through the rolled tongue.

"To be in balance, it's essential to have the breath in balance. When we're angry, the exhalation tends to be stronger than the inhalation. When we're sad, the inhalation tends to be stronger than the exhalation. When we're feeling fear, we don't breathe much at all. By bringing the breath back into balance . . . it helps bring our life back into balance."

—DAN MILLMAN

"The soul should always stand ajar, ready to welcome the ecstatic experience."
—EMILY DICKINSON

Exercise 8

Breath of Fire: Kapalabhati—Skull Shining

The translation of the word "kapalabhati" tells a lot about the technique. *Kapal* means "skull," and *bhati* is "light," or "luster." In essence, the technique works to brighten the mind with light and cleanse the body with heat.

This is not only one of the most beneficial techniques, it is also one that looks unusual. In fact, when beginners are instructed to do this technique in a yoga class, they often think, "You've got to be kidding." However, those who move beyond this initial reaction are always glad they did.

The technique is done in a kneeling or seated position. Place your hands palms down on your thighs, straighten your spine, and allow your shoulders to relax.

Take in a deep inhalation, breathing through the nose. As you exhale, contract your lower abdominal musculature with a powerful push. Work from inside your belly, quickly directing your abdomen back against your spine to help expel the air. The exhalation is forceful and the inhalation is passive. Each exhalation is fast—about one second—and is repeated twenty to forty times. Inhalations come naturally between the exhalations. If you feel dizzy, stop the exercise.

The technique strengthens the respiratory system and the abdominal wall. It invigorates the entire system as the heat it generates helps to cleanse the body and bring clarity to the mind.

Exercise 9

A l t e r n a t e   N o s t r i l   B r e a t h i n g — A n a l o m a   V i l o m a

Called by different names, this technique is considered the king of the pranayamas. It is excellent for balancing energies. Some say it balances the male and female within; others say it equalizes the emotional with the physical. It creates a feeling of quick vitality and calms the mind.

The optimal breathing method employs a one-four-two count in which you in-

Coordinating Breath and Movement

In yoga, breath and movement go together just like the old song says love and marriage do: "like a horse and carriage." When you begin to link breath and movement, here are a few basics to keep in mind:

✦ Inhalations and exhalations are linked to the direction in which the spine or limbs move. Once you integrate this into your practice, it will exemplify the true path of yoga— the practice of joining together—which in this case is the union of movement and breath.

✦ Inhalations work best with upward or expanding movements. For example, if you are lying on your belly and begin to raise your head, chest, and upper back to come into the Cobra pose, your breath will be on the inhale during that movement. If you hold the pose, your breath will be rhythmic, including even inhalations and exhalations.

✦ As you lower your chest and head, allowing the spine to straighten, you'll find that the exhalation is a natural part of the movement. That's because exhalations are coordinated with contracting, downward movements. An exception here is in raising the legs, which is also accompanied by an exhalation. Whenever you twist the spine or bend forward, your breath will want to be released.

Listen to these natural cues, as they offer sound advice.

hale for a count of four seconds, hold for a count of sixteen, and exhale for a count of eight. Try to follow this, but if you can't, just stick to whatever count is comfortable.

On your right hand, fold your index finger and your middle finger easily toward your palm. Extend your right thumb. Now gently hold the right thumb against your right nostril and inhale through your left nostril. Fill your lungs with the inhalation, allowing every little crevice to be touched by breath.

After you have inhaled—and your right thumb is still pressed against your right nostril—swing your ring finger over to your left nostril and hold it closed. Both nostrils are now held closed with the right hand. Hold them closed for as long as you comfortably can.

To exhale, lift your right thumb from your right nostril and allow the exhalation to travel through the right nostril, emptying the lungs. Once the exhalation is complete, inhale through the right nostril. The left nostril remains closed, as the ring finger is still pressed against it.

Again, hold the breath. For this exhalation, open the left nostril, and then inhale on the left side. Repeat this sequence ten times.

As you develop the proper, conscious use of breath, you will discover that this very simple act is key to feeling balanced, strong, and energized.

SUGGESTED READING

Hanh, Thich Nhat. *Breathe! You Are Alive: Sutra on the Full Awareness of Breathing.* Berkeley, Ca.: Parallax, 1990.

Iyengar, B. K. S. *Light on Pranayama: The Yogic Art of Breathing.* New York: Crossroads, 1995.

Mohan, A. G., and Miller, Kathleen (eds.). *Yoga for Body, Breath, and Mind: A Guide to Personal Reintegration.* Portland, Oreg: Rudra, 1995.

Swami Rama, Rudolph Ballentine, M.D., Alan Hymes, M.D. *Science of Breath: A Practical Guide.* The Himalayan International Institute.

Moving into Postures

6

As a beginner, moving into postures—even the ones that look simple in the illustrations—may feel intimidating. One reason is because you are embarking on a new journey, which always takes courage. Another reason is that yoga holds a lot of promises. This book, and other materials you may have read, describes the benefits of yoga both on and off the mat. As you begin your practice, focus less on what you may eventually reap by becoming a yogi and more on how each asana—or posture—feels in your body, in the moment.

Before trying any pose, take the time to read all the way through the instructions. Let your eyes rest on the illustration. Look at the placement of the spine, the shoulders, the neck, the knees, the feet. As you practice the pose yourself, allow your thoughts to scan your body, checking for places where you might be holding tension. Are your shoulders up by your ears? Are you breathing? Breath brings oxygen to the muscles, so they do not tire as quickly and you have the energy you need to enjoy your practice.

Allow yourself to recognize how you are feeling as you start out—and then to accept these feelings. Think about what you need to adjust, and make the adjustments easily. When you begin yoga, it isn't about doing it right. It's about doing it consciously.

Here are a few guidelines to help you as you begin your yoga practice:

- Breathe.

- Keep your eyes open, your gaze soft for standing postures, but closed when you can.

- Explore the balance of respecting your limits while still challenging yourself.

- Enjoy yourself.

- Move slowly, with intention.

- Listen to your body.

- Relax.

- Breathe.

Postures

Warm-ups

Warm-up postures are designed to do exactly that: warm you up. These postures combine stretches, toning, and flexibility. You may be moving in new ways, so take the time to go slowly and develop an at-home familiarity with your body.

Neck Rolls

Neck Rolls are an important way to begin to practice because of the tension that most of us carry in the neck and shoulders. The neck is a sensitive area, so explore these movements slowly. Neck Rolls are helpful not only at the beginning of a full yoga practice but can be done in an office or whenever a brief stress-buster break is needed.

- Sit in a chair with your spine straight, both feet flat on the floor or legs crossed easily if sitting on floor.

- With your arms resting easily at your sides, palms facing inward, inhale slowly and lift your shoulders up to your earlobes. Exhaling, lower them slowly back down.

- Roll the shoulders now, making circles toward the front and the back. Allow your arms to follow the rolling movement. Repeat this three times, slowly, breathing mindfully. Remember, the goal is not to get through the practice but to savor it.

- After several rolls, sit still for a moment, feeling the renewed energy you have just brought to your shoulders. Now imagine a string attached to the crown of your head, stretching you up just a little taller. Feel the lengthening in the back of the neck.

+ Exhaling, bend your head forward, lowering your chin toward your neck. Keep your spine upright. As you exhale, visualize any feelings of tension or worries leaving your neck and shoulders.

+ Inhaling, lift your head, feeling it float just a little bit higher on your neck. Direct your inhalation into your upper back, shoulders, and upper rib cage.

+ Repeat three times. Your arms remain resting at your sides, but as the energy begins to flow you may begin to feel a tingling in your fingers.

+ Again, sit still for a moment, feeling the softness in your face, the relaxed glow of your upper body. Bring hands to a resting position, palms facing up on thighs or on legs. Inhaling, drop your chin forward and let the head roll all the way around, in a big circle, as you exhale. Roll your head to the right three times and to the left three times, stopping for a moment to center yourself between sides.

+ After the final Neck Roll, sit quietly, breathing fully.

Cat and Dog Stretch

The Cat and Dog Stretch allows you to experience the range of motion of the spine—it actually massages the muscles in your back—and the placement of the pelvis. It also strengthens your arms and helps to flatten the stomach.

How to do the pose:

+ In a kneeling position, lean forward and place your hands on the floor directly underneath your shoulders and your knees directly under your hips.

> "If anything is sacred, the human body is sacred."
> —WALT WHITMAN

+ Spread your fingers apart, thighs and arms perpendicular to the ground. Your spine should be lengthened and parallel to the floor. Keep the back of your neck long and extended, and your face looking toward the floor.

+ On the inhale, lift both your chin and your tailbone up, arching the spine. This is the Dog Stretch, and should make a saddle in your back.

+ On the exhale, round your spine, lifting your navel up, into your belly, while moving your tailbone and head back down. Make sure you begin the rounding process by first tucking in your tailbone. This is called the Cat Stretch.

+ Repeat this several times, coordinating with the breath each time. Take a moment to experience the fluid, sequential movement of your spine. You might experiment with the breath here, pausing to hold the inhalation as you arch and then pausing again as you fully exhale, pulling your belly up and in when you round the spine.

When you finish the repetitions, check to see that your shoulder blades are separate, the facial muscles passive, and the throat open.

Forearm Stretch

This is a nice way to wake up your arms. It is especially useful after working with your hands—whether at the keyboard or the carpentry bench.

How to do the pose:

- Sit in a kneeling position on the floor, with your buttocks comfortably resting on your heels.
- Place your hands on the floor in front of you, turned so that the tips of your fingers graze your knees.
- Flatten your palms against the floor. You should feel a stretch at this point.
- Keep your shoulders rolled back and down.
- Be careful not to raise your buttocks up in order to flatten your palms.
- If you cannot flatten the palms, simply press them toward the floor until you feel a stretch.
- If you can flatten the palms, lean back slightly to increase the stretch.
- Finish by sitting back on your heels for a moment, shake out your hands, and then notice the energy you have just brought to your arms.

Butterfly Pose—Baddha Konasana

The Butterfly pose opens the hip joints and loosens the hips and ankles. Some say its name comes from the image of a butterfly resting on its wings.

How to do the pose:

♦ Sit on the floor and bring the soles of your feet together. Your soles should touch one another just as your palms do in prayer. Clasp your feet with your hands, keeping the soles together, and draw them gently toward your body. You may not be able to bring them in very close, which is fine.

- Open your chest by pushing your shoulder blades together and press your knees toward the floor. If your knees are far off the floor, resist bouncing them up and down. Gravity will work its own magic on opening up your hip joints.

- Hold this position as you breathe with evenly measured inhalations and exhalations. Eventually you may be able to bend forward, but right now simply feel the opening at the hip joint.

There are two ways to work with your spine when you practice this pose:

- In one, your entire back is straight. You may need to tilt your lower back inward to align the spine. If you feel your upper back rounding, you can leave your feet farther out from your body.

- In another, you can roll your spine, dropping your head and rounding your upper back.

Salutation to the Sun—Surya Namaskara

Here's an energizing way to start the day. The Salutation to the Sun is a series of twelve fluid postures that journey through pose and counterpose, giving you an easy, energizing workout. It is a favorite of beginners and oldtime yogis alike.

Though you can add additional stretches or poses, it's a good idea to learn the sequences as described here and then add variety as you feel secure in the basic routine.

How to do the Salutation to the Sun:

POSE I: MOUNTAIN POSE

Stand with your feet planted firmly on the floor. Spread your toes. Pause to feel yourself connected to that spot, clearing your mind for the practice. Relax your face and neck. Open your chest, rolling your shoulders back and down. Keep your legs strong—you can do this by tightening the muscles of the thighs, lifting the kneecaps, and tightening the buttocks. Wait for a moment, listening for your internal cue to begin.

Then bring your hands together in a prayer position, palms together in front of your heart. Exhale.

POSE 2: STANDING BACK BEND

Inhaling, separate your hands and raise your arms up above your head as you arch back. Keep your fingers pointed as you let your arms reach slightly behind you.

As you arch your back, tighten your buttocks muscles to protect your lower back and keep your feet firmly on the floor. Think of your pelvis as your center of stability as your upper body reaches up and away from your solid stance.

POSE 3: STANDING FORWARD BEND

Exhaling, bring your arms all the way down to the floor. You can bend your knees if that is more comfortable. Place your hands outside of your feet or grab your heels. If you can flatten the palms, do so, but the experience is just as satisfying even if your fingertips only brush the floor.

Let your head dangle, relaxing your neck and shoulders. At the same time, keep your legs strong, taking care not to lock your knees, and keep your feet firmly planted.

POSE 4: LEFT LUNGE

Inhaling, rest your palms flat against the floor. Be prepared for them to take some weight.

Bend your knees and stretch your right leg back. Your left leg will be bent directly over your left foot, keeping your knee in line with your ankle. Your thigh will be as closely parallel to the ground as possible. Your right leg will be straight behind you, toes flexed like a sprinter.

Raise your face, looking up, and push your chest slightly between your arms. Keep your expression relaxed. There should be a straight line between your shoulders and your left heel.

POSE 5: PLANK POSE

Exhaling, now bring your left leg back alongside your right leg. It may feel like you are in gym class again, about to do a round of push-ups. Keep your back and buttocks in a straight line, so that you actually become the plank.

Look down between your hands as you maintain this position, and keep your abdominal muscles firm. Take a deep breath and prepare to move into the next pose.

POSE 6: EIGHT-POINT POSE

Exhaling, come out of the fifth pose by bending your knees to the floor, then bending your arms and lowering your chest and chin, also all the way to the floor. This transition may feel awkward at first, but with practice it will begin to flow smoothly. Your back will be arched, your buttocks raised. Keep your toes curled.

POSE 7: UPWARD DOG

Inhaling, lower your hips, raise your chest, and straighten your arms. If you can, try to do this in one smooth motion. Your back will be arched, your legs together and extending fully behind you. Keep your toes tucked. Broaden the chest and roll your shoulders back and down. Look upward, extending the lift of the chest.

POSE 8: DOWNWARD DOG

Exhaling, raise your knees off the floor and, keeping your legs straight, lift your hips up and back and lean forward onto your hands, which are palm down on the floor. Your body should be in an upside-down **V** shape. Point your buttocks up so your whole body is feeling the stretch. Let your head hang, and make sure your neck and shoulders are relaxed. Just as they did in the Standing Back Bend, your hips create the stability in this pose. Press your palms and feet into the floor. Press your chest toward the floor.

POSE 9: RIGHT LUNGE

This is the counterpose to Pose 4, the Left Lunge. Inhaling, let your palms rest flat on the floor and prepared to take some weight.

Bend your knees and stretch your left leg back. Your right leg will be bent, knee directly in line with ankle and your right foot will be a solid anchor. Your left leg will be straight behind you, your left foot flexed like a sprinter's.

Raise your face, looking up, and push your chest slightly between your arms. Keep your face soft and relaxed. There should be a straight line between your shoulders and your right heel.

POSE 10: STANDING FORWARD BEND

Exhaling, straighten your legs so you are standing with your arms and your upper body hanging down toward the floor as you did in Pose 3. You can bend your knees,

and, if possible, let your head rest against them. At this point in the routine your legs may feel more energized than they did during the first forward bend, so be especially mindful of keeping them firm. Feel your feet securely on the ground.

POSE 11: STANDING BACK BEND

We're about to complete the cycle now. Inhaling, lift your hands off the floor and stretch your arms all the way over your head, bending back from the hips. Remember to tighten your buttocks muscles to protect your lower back. Look out through your hands, which are apart. Your palms are facing each other. Stay centered, keeping your hips directly over your feet as you stretch back.

POSE 12: MOUNTAIN POSE

Exhaling, let your arms come back to the prayer position, palms together in front of the heart. Pause here. Look straight ahead, your gaze soft, your face relaxed. You've just offered your body a wonderful experience. Relish the feeling of energy and serenity. Allow any swirling thoughts to settle in your mind. Take a few deep breaths and start the Salutation to the Sun again, this time moving back with the alternate leg.

Repeat this three times every morning.

Knee to Chest Pose—Apanasana

Apana is the Sanskrit word for "descending breath." This posture is associated with the lower body and exhalation. The pose can be done passively to massage the internal organs or can be active, offering a good stretch to the lower back and hip joints.

The pose is described here with a few variations, each of which help to tone the abdominal muscles and enhance flexibility in the spine.

How to do the pose:

- Lie on your back, taking a moment to feel the weight of your body against the mat or blanket. Take a few slow, relaxing breaths, allowing time for the mind to become still and the body centered.

- Exhaling, bring your right thigh toward your chest. As you raise it up and fold it against your chest, include the left leg in your awareness. Keep this leg straight, with the foot flexed.

- Clasp your hands together over your right knee, entwining your fingers. This will pull the right leg snuggly to your chest.

- Hold this position for several breaths. You may feel a stretch in your thigh and the rise and fall of your belly against your right leg. Keep your spine flat against the floor.

- Take advantage of this relaxed pose to inhale and exhale deeply, fully experiencing the widening of your rib cage.

- After a few breaths, extend your right leg back down to lie straight alongside the left leg. Feel the difference in each leg and hip joint. Breathe here for a moment before starting the posture on the other side.

- Bring both knees to the chest, squeezing them against your body. Take deep breaths, feeling the deep massage of your internal organs.

- Finish by extending the legs and taking in a few breaths. Feel your weight against the floor.

Variations

OPEN KNEE TO SIDE

- Lying down, extend the left arm out to the left at shoulder level. Your palm will be facing the floor and fingers spread.

- Bend the right leg and place the right foot on the floor next to the left knee.

- Exhaling, rest your right hand on your right knee and guide it gently out to the side toward the floor. Feel the opening in your hip joint, and allow the waist to lift slightly from the floor.

- Be mindful of the placement of your hips, as they should remain squared toward the ceiling. Your left leg should be straight, the foot flexed.

- Feel the opening and relaxation of the hip joint.

- Exhaling, lift the knee back to center. Straighten the right leg. Sense the difference between the two hip joints, taking a moment to sense the opening you just created, before practicing the pose on the left side.

KNEE DOWN TWIST

This is a wonderful way to stretch the torso, and tone the waist.

- Lie on your back with your legs together flat on the floor.

- Extend your arms out to the side, forming a cross.

- Inhaling, bend your right leg and place your right foot on top of your left knee.

- Exhaling, move the right knee to the left across your extended leg and press the knee down toward the floor. You can get help in lowering your right knee by using your left hand to press the right knee down.

+ Keep your shoulders on the floor and turn your head to face your right hand, which will remain palm down on the floor. You will feel a stretch in the spine, shoulder, and upper arm area.

+ Breathe into the spinal twist, observing how the tension along your back and in your belly loosens with each inhalation and exhalation.

+ After a few breaths, lift your right leg back to the center of your torso and straighten it out on the floor. Feel the full width of your back against the mat. Bring your awareness to your torso, feeling the difference between the two sides. Begin the twist on the opposite side.

Standing Postures

7

Standing poses strengthen the legs, improve balance and alignment, and increase the flexibility in hip joints and the spine. And because of the importance that "taking a stand" has in our lives, these postures bring more to us than their effect on our bodies.

Think about all the casual references we have to standing in our everyday speech. When you are just starting out in the working world, you look forward to the day when you can "stand on your own two feet." When you believe in something, you "take a stand"; when you want something, you "put your best foot forward"; and when you feel nervous, you might have "jelly legs." When your life becomes difficult, have you ever heard yourself saying you "just can't stand it anymore"? We bring a lot of meaning to the ordinary act of standing.

The way we stand can say a lot about how we feel, as well, even if we are not aware of it. Next time you are waiting at the kitchen sink, just letting the soapy water cover the dishes, pause to check out your posture—or, in other words, your stance. Is one

---

"Stand through life firm as a rock in the sea,
undisturbed and unmoved by its ever rising waves."

—HAZRAT INAYAT KAHN

---

shoulder higher than the other? Is one hip carrying more weight? Are your shoulders stooped, or is your lower back tight? How does your body feel?

The yoga postures that follow all work with standing postures to develop stability and focus and help increase range of movement. They will also bring you into a close connection with what it means to take a stand, to be in balance, and to stand on your own two feet.

If you find yourself wobbling, try focusing on your center. Imagine the strength that emanates up from the earth and through the core of your very being.

Postures

Mountain Pose—Tadasana

Though the Mountain pose may look like it is just a matter of standing still, it's actually a serious posture and requires great concentration to do well. In fact, the fundamentals of placement and alignment in tadasana are important to understand because they carry into all the other poses.

The word *tadasana* means "standing straight like a mountain." The challenge of the pose is in balancing the body. As you stand in tadasana, try to create a foundation of stability and symmetry, just like a mountain.

How to do the pose:

+ Put your feet together with your toes pointing forward. The big toes should touch and the heels should touch.

"Give me a place to stand and I will move the world."
—ARCHIMEDES

+ Check to see that your body weight is evenly distributed between the heels and the balls of your feet, and on each side.

+ Breathe easily, allowing the lower ribs to expand on the inhalation. Think about letting all tensions release as you feel yourself grounded to this spot, standing firmly.

+ Allow your arms to hang at your sides, palms facing toward your body.

The next instructions are designed to enhance the sensation of being firmly connected to the ground, like a mountain:

+ While remaining in a relaxed state, breathing easily, lift the arches of the feet, engage the calf and thigh muscles by pressing the muscle in toward the bone, and lift the kneecaps.

+ Tighten your buttocks muscles to protect the lower back and tuck your tailbone under, automatically lifting the hipbones so they face forward like two headlights. This brings the pelvis into proper alignment.

+ Lift and extend out of the waist, pulling the stomach muscles up and in.

+ Lift the sternum, roll your shoulders back and down, bring your chin parallel to the floor, press out of the crown of your head, and lengthen the back of the neck.

+ Lengthen the arms all the way out through the fingertips.

+ Your throat and facial muscles should be soft.

+ As you inhale, lift your arms overhead until they are fully extended. Palms face each other.

+ Hold for ten seconds and then on an exhalation lower the arms back down to your sides.

+ Repeat three times.

- Pause to sense the stability and balance throughout your body. These feelings are key to performing all standing postures.

Swinging Twist

This is a fun, gentle warm-up for the spine, the legs, and the belly.
How to do the pose:

- Stand with your feet a few inches wider than your shoulders. Let your arms hang down as if they were empty coat sleeves.

- Gently swing your arms side to side, allowing your torso to follow the impulse of the movement. Look over your shoulder with each twist, as if you are looking at someone or something behind you.

- If you are turning your body to the left, swinging your arms to the left side, and looking over your left shoulder, direct your right knee toward your left side. This will create a corkscrew effect.

- Repeat this motion in a fluid, easy rhythm.

- When you have practiced this for a few minutes, stand in the Mountain pose and center yourself with several deep breaths.

It is important to be aware of alignment as you stretch your arms to the side in the Half Moon. You may remember an exercise like this one in an early gym class in which you were instructed to bend your arms all the way to the side, your head drooping down toward the floor. That exercise encouraged you to fold your torso over at the waist, pushing against the rib cage.

The Half Moon pose is about stretching and extending, not bending. The difference has to do with opening up and lengthening the rib cage instead of folding over it. Therefore, as you bend to the right side and your arms reach up and out, make sure that the stretch your left side enjoys is not at the expense of a collapsed right torso.

It is also important not to let the arms dangle back or swing forward but to keep them framed above the center of the body.

Half Moon Pose—Ardha Chandrasana

The Half Moon pose gives you a chance to get a nice stretch while maintaining the foundation and stability of the Mountain pose. Playing with the opposite directions that the Half Moon travels in—stretching to the side while staying rooted to the ground—is a good exploration of strength and flexibility.

The pose also teaches you to remain in one plane, heightening your awareness of how your body moves in space.

"Yoga positions are entered and held by the body in order to find the peace within—the point where sustaining the pose is easy, natural and feels 'right.' The more difficult the pose, the harder it is to find peace. Yoga postures mirror life. When things are easy, it's easy to feel good. But feeling good when things aren't going your way—whether it's a bad hair day or a more serious tragedy—is a challenge. Yoga is a journey through the poses, working with each pose until you find that peace, then progressing to the next level. This progression combines the building of physical strength with the toning of the mind."

—*THE COMPLETE IDIOT'S GUIDE TO YOGA* BY JOAN BUDILOVSKY AND EVE ADAMSON

The Half Moon pose tones the abdominal muscles, rejuvenates the adrenal glands, and expands the lung capacity.

How to do the pose:

+ Begin in the Mountain pose.

+ Inhale, lift your arms so that palms face inward, and reach above your head. Touch your fingers together, cross your thumbs, and extend the arms up— as if you are making a church steeple. Broaden the chest and roll your shoulders back and down. Keep your arms and fingers extended as you reach toward the sky.

+ Keep your chin level. Shoulders will lift naturally, so be aware of this and lower them back down. Try not to let them raise up around your ears. Relax your face, neck, throat, and eyes.

+ Keep your pelvis level and your legs strong. Lift your kneecaps, tighten the buttocks, and allow the spine to extend out of the hips.

+ Take a moment to feel the stretch using mindful, carefully paced breaths.

+ With the arms extended and the legs firm, bend over to one side. Keep your torso lifted so that you are lengthening the underneath side of the rib cage. Keep your neck and head extended. Try for a smooth curve from the sole of your heel to the tip of your fingers. You are stretching up and over—you

are not pointing your hands back down to the floor. It is easy for your arms to sway toward the front or back at this point, so check to make sure they are centered. Keep your hands, hips, and shoulders aligned in one plane.

+ Hold here and breathe. Repeat on the other side, but each time you switch sides, take a moment to pause at center to scan your body, checking in to see if you have remained grounded or are off balance.

Tree Pose—Vrikshasana

The Tree pose is a wonderful teacher, as you have the opportunity to explore how each side of the body works with stability and balance. It works with concentration, strengthens equilibrium, and promotes character and willpower.

How to do the pose:

+ Start in the Mountain pose. Breathe easily until you feel both feet squarely on the ground and a solid, grounded sense of your center.

+ Inhaling, shift your weight to the left leg.

+ Exhaling, bend your right leg, clasping the ankle with your right hand and placing the right foot on the inside of the left thigh. Though you will even-

tually want to place the foot as high up as you can, when you first start out you can place it above the knee. The right knee should be extending out to the side.

+ Place your hands either above your head, fingers together and thumbs crossed—again, as if you are making a shape like a steeple—or over your heart in a prayer position.

+ Maintain a sense of strength and stability in your standing leg, keeping the foot firmly against the floor, the knee straight and the thigh firm.

+ At the same time, survey your posture to make sure your hips are square and open, buttocks firm, your lower back tucked in, and the front of the torso lifted and strong. Dropping your bent knee away from the hip may help to lengthen your waist.

+ Because the pose is challenging, it is easy for the shoulders to hunch up— make sure they are relaxed. Soften the face, eyes, and throat, as well.

+ Pause, holding your balance before repeating on the other side. When you are ready to try the other side, let your arms float gently down to your sides and return to Mountain pose, finding your own centered, steady mountain before repeating the Tree pose.

As a beginner, you may find that maintaining your balance in the Tree pose is a real challenge. This is natural—in fact, even longtime yogis can be wobbly trees. To gain the most from this pose, allow your focus to help you. Concentrate on your internal center, located two inches below the navel, while you allow your external gaze to rest on one point. Yogis call this internal center the hara point and consider it to be the source of willpower and intention. You may be amazed at how easily this steadies you during the pose. You might also think about how the pose is like a tree, with your legs rooted to the ground and your arms reaching up, like two strong branches pointed toward the sky.

Acquiring the ability to balance yourself with a strong focus is an important skill to bring into other parts of your life, as well.

Shoulder Stretch

This is an excellent pose for anyone who spends time at the keyboard, as it allows the shoulder area to open up and helps to prevent rotator cuff injuries. It is also stretches the back and the hamstrings.

How to do the pose:

+ Stand about two feet from the wall. Raise your hands and place them against the wall, positioned above your head.

+ Press your sternum toward the floor. Arch your back, pressing your buttocks out behind you and pressing your underarms toward the wall. You will feel a stretch along the back of your legs.

+ Roll your shoulders back and down. You can either drop your head or keep your head up, with your ears parallel between your arms.

+ Hold this position for several breaths, feeling the stretch across your shoulder area.

Triangle Pose—Trikonasana

Like the Tree, the Triangle is a pose that may take some getting used to, but it is a joy to practice once you feel at home with it.

The pose is exactly what its Sanskrit name says it is: *tri* is "three," and *kona* means "angle." The Triangle pose strengthens the legs, enhances flexibility in the hips, and tones the muscles of the torso. And because there is a lot going on in this pose, practicing it with care takes concentration and awareness, so it enhances these skills, as well.

How to do the pose:

+ From the Mountain pose, spread the feet about three to three and a half feet apart. Lift your arms so they are level with your shoulders, parallel to the floor, keeping your palms down.

+ Turn your left foot in 30 degrees, and turn your right foot out 90 degrees. Your right heel should be in line with the arch of your left foot.

+ Take a moment to look at the placement of your knees. Keep your legs straight and kneecaps lifted by engaging your thighs. Make sure your right knee is in line with your right foot.

Inhale as you scan your body, feeling steady and strong in your wide stance.

+ Exhaling, shift your pelvis to the left as you reach your hand toward the right, as if you wanted the fingertips on your right hand to touch a spot a few feet away. Keep the stretch open and lifted, as it was in the Half Moon pose. Look forward.

+ Working with the stretch of your right arm, lower your right hand and place it in front of your right shin or ankle, palm facing away. As you reach down

"Nothing happens until something moves."
—ALBERT EINSTEIN

with your right arm, raise the left arm straight above your head, fingertips pointing to the ceiling, palm facing out.

+ Be mindful of your back leg, as it is easy to divert your attention from it as you position your arms and experience the side stretch. Don't let it flop inward at this point. Push down on your back heel to keep the leg actively involved in the posture.

+ Shift your gaze toward your left thumb by turning your head. Keep your trunk lateral, taking care not to bend forward or tilt back. Hold this posi-

tion, breathing rhythmically to support the pose. Imagine your shoulders, hands, hips, and feet in one plane between two panes of Plexiglas.

+ Coming out of the pose, turn your head back so you are looking forward. You might need to bend the knee slightly at this point. Inhale as you come upright, then exhale as you turn your right foot forward.

+ Return to the Mountain pose before initiating the pose on the other side.

Here's an example of how a simple prop can make all the difference in gaining the most from a posture. If you have difficulty balancing, or if reaching your shin or ankle is uncomfortable, try placing a wooden block behind your front foot and placing your hand on the top of this block instead of on your shin or ankle. This will allow you to achieve the stretch and strengthening of the torso without any distracting discomfort in the legs.

Warrior Pose—Virabhadrasana

The warrior in this pose trains to conquer inner turmoil, working toward peace and serenity. The pose fills the body with nobility and strength. As the arms reach toward the sun and the feet are planted firmly on earth, the center is solid, the heart open.

The Warrior pose supports deep breathing, relieves stiffness in the neck and shoulders, strengthens the legs, and tones the hips and buttocks.

As always, check in with yourself for a moment before you begin the pose. Are you about to practice the Warrior pose with a feeling of battle fatigue from a long day? If so, give yourself a few more minutes to stand in the Mountain pose first. A true warrior brings a quiet mind and a clear spirit.

"Your vision will become clear only when you look into your heart.
Who looks outside, dreams. Who looks inside, awakens."

—CARL JUNG

How to do the pose:

+ Moving from the Mountain pose, spring one foot forward about three to four feet. Inhaling, bring your arms up over your head, palms facing each other. Interlace your fingers with the index fingers pointing up and the thumbs crossed. Drop your shoulders.

+ Root the weight in the back leg. Keep your gaze forward and steady.

+ Exhaling, bend your front knee until your thigh is parallel to the floor. Keep your knee in line with your ankle. Take care not to lunge. Extend the back leg straight behind you with toes curled under. Lengthen the spine out from the hips and press out of the crown of your head. Focus on a point in front of you to keep balanced.

+ You may feel a stretch on both the front thigh and the calf of your back leg. As you feel this stretch, push down slightly on your back heel. Feel the upward lift of your torso and the downward pull of your legs.

+ Breathe fully, opening up your rib cage. Extend the spine upward, toward the fingers, keeping the chest broad and the shoulders rolled and back down. Look up toward the ceiling. Hold the pose for a few seconds longer than you think you can, drawing on the strong intention within.

Balancing Stick Pose—Tuladanasana

Here's another opportunity to bring balance into your life. This posture helps to develop control and concentration, and also strengthens the legs and tones the abdominal muscles. It's great for improving posture, as well.

As with the Tree pose, the Balancing Stick requires an even-keeled mind. In this case, once the focus wanders, the pose transforms from a balancing stick to a swaying one. This is natural, especially at first. As you continue to practice, you will discover that holding the pose and feeling the stretch and strengthening becomes a matter of intent. And like so many yoga postures, the ability to focus, balance, and maintain a steady stand on the mat will show up subtly in your life.

How to do the pose:

+ Beginning in the Mountain pose, stretch your arms up above your head and bring your palms together. Interlace your fingers. Cross your thumbs, and point the index fingers up as if you are forming the steeple of a church.

+ Step forward about two feet with your right leg. Place your left toe back, positioned to lift and point behind you. Focus your gaze on one spot on the floor a short distance away.

+ Prepare to bend forward. Sense the grounded, rooted quality of the right leg. Pivot at your hips, bending at your waist, moving the back, head, and outstretched arms in one smooth motion and bringing them parallel to the ground.

- As you lower your upper body, you will lift the left leg back and straight, pointing the toes behind you. Your head should stay level with your arms. Your body is in one horizontal line above your right leg, forming a T.

- The top of your body, from the tips of your fingers to the end of your toes, in one straight line, is now being balanced on your right leg.

- Bring your attention to the right leg and buttock. Pull up through the muscles to keep them engaged, but take care not to lock the knee. Keep your navel pulled up toward your spine and press your weight slightly forward, following the reach of your arms, to help your leg remain steady.

- There is a lot going on right now, so remember to breathe mindfully.

- Hold the pose for about ten seconds. Once you are able to hold it comfortably, allow yourself to float above your leg longer, savoring your inner focus and strength.

- Repeat on the other side, but give yourself a chance to come back to the Mountain pose and feel both feet securely on the ground before switching sides.

Standing Head to Knee—Dandayamana-Janushirasana

This pose helps to develop concentration, patience, and determination. It is also good for toning the abdominal and thigh muscles and improves the flexibility of sciatic nerves.

How to do the pose:

- Stand in Tadasana with arms at your sides.

- Lift your right knee and, bending forward, take hold of the right foot with both hands, interlacing fingers under the foot; your thumbs should be on the toes.

- Straighten your standing leg, keeping thigh muscles tight. Extend the held leg in front of you, pulling the ball of your foot and your toes toward you.

- Now prepare to focus on balance. Straighten your leg out parallel to the floor. You will naturally lean over the leg. Keep your elbows pointed to the floor.

- Direct energy down through your standing leg, creating a firm connection to the ground.

- To create a more challenging pose, focus your gaze on one point on the floor and increase the bend of your torso over the extended leg. See if you can touch your forehead to your knee. If you can do this without strain, breathe normally and keep this position for ten counts.

- Remember, keep your gaze steady. This will help you to maintain your balance in this pose.

King of the Dancers—Natrajanasana

The King of the Dancers energizes the body by working with complementary opposites. The posture transfers circulation from one side of the body to the other and then equalizes it, pumping fresh blood throughout and rejuvenating the organs and glands.

The pose works with balance, concentration, patience, and stability. Physically, it firms the abdominal wall and upper thighs, tightens the upper arms, and expands the rib cage. As its name suggests, the position turns your body into the shape of a bow —the kind of bow that is used to shoot an arrow.

How to do the pose:

+ From the Mountain pose, move your weight onto your left leg. Feel yourself maintaining balance in your center while you shift your weight.

+ Reach your right arm up toward the ceiling and sweep it behind you, opening the shoulder area. Your right hand is now palm open, facing to the outside and behind you.

+ Bend your right knee and lift your right foot, clasping it with your right hand. Your weight is on your left leg. Find your balance.

+ The way in which you hold your right foot has an impact on your shoulder joint, so take a moment to make sure you are doing it correctly. Your right

hand should grasp the instep about two inches below the toes. Your wrist should be inside the foot, your fingers pointing outward, the sole of your foot facing the ceiling. In other words, do not allow the arm and hand to be on the outside of the foot.

+ Breathe evenly to support the movement.

+ Lift your left arm in front of you, pointing forward. Focus on a spot in line with your left hand.

+ Maintaining your steady balance on your left leg, roll your body forward — think of rolling like a wheel—working toward getting your abdomen parallel to the floor. Be mindful of the left leg, as this is a transition in which it can be easy to lock the knee. Keep it engaged by pulling up on the thigh.

+ Raise your right foot up as you reach forward with your left arm, extending the stretch in your torso.

+ Hold this pose for a count of five, breathing fully. After you bring the right leg down, center yourself in the Mountain pose before beginning the standing bow on the opposite side.

As you become familiar with the posture and ready to explore it more fully, imagine yourself being strung and drawn by an archer. This requires bringing your head and spine back as you pivot forward, creating a curve in your back. Take care not to pinch your back, and be mindful of the tension in the knee of your standing leg.

Think about the amount of time a champion archer takes to steady the bow, zero in on the target, and sense the pressure in his string before he shoots. Take the same kind of care as you journey into the posture. Move slowly and consciously, bringing attention to each motion and its impact on the overall pose.

8.

Floor Postures

The following postures take you to the floor, where you can explore a variety of stretches, spinal twists, back bends, inversions, and centering.

Child's Pose—Mudhasana

Here's a pleasurable way to spend a few minutes. Despite its name (*bala* means "child" in Sanskrit), this pose is a welcome treat for yogis and yoginis of all ages, whether resting after a difficult pose or relaxing in the middle of a busy day.

The Child's pose relieves lower back tension, brings circulation to the lower back and belly, and tones the pelvic area. If you feel resistance in your knees, try placing a blanket underneath them for support and a pillow between your thighs and calves.

How to do the pose:

"What you cannot find in your body you will not find anywhere else."

—ASIAN PROVERB

- Start out on your hands and knees. Relax here for a minute, just breathing easily.

- Exhaling, sit back on your heels. Rest your forehead on the floor, chest to knees.

- Your shoulders may drop here. Feel the release at the top of your spine, between the shoulder blades, as you allow your arms to rest heavily on the floor. Try breathing into this space between your shoulder blades, bringing your attention to loosening the muscles along your spine.

- Hold the pose for several breaths, enjoying the relaxation.

- To come out of the pose, simply roll your back up slowly, place your hands on your lap and sit quietly. Scan your back, from your neck to your buttocks, to see if any tension remains.

For variation, try these two alternatives:

- Sit on your heels with your forehead on the floor, arms stretched out on the floor in front of you.

- Inhale, and as you exhale lift your buttocks slightly and slide your arms forward, lifting your forehead off the floor.

- Another variation you can try if your stomach feels uncomfortable in the other poses is as follows. First, when you are on your hands and knees, bring your big toes together and widen you knees. Now draw the buttocks back to the heels and lean forward over your thighs, relaxing your entire back. Fold your arms on the floor in front of you so that just the area between your elbows and wrists rests on the floor. Lower your forehead to your hands.

"Tremendous emotional energy is expended because we are ignorant of, or afraid of and therefore denying, what we feel at any moment. The sensation of stretching and opening is the focus of the asana, unlike most of our waking moments when we are expected to ignore our physical sensations. The wonderful paradox of awareness is that when we become truly aware of what is, things begin to change. All other approaches to sensation are forms of running away. For no other reason than this, asana practice can be a wonderful antidote to the stress of modern life."

—JUDITH LASATER, PH.D.

Leg Assisted Tie—Supra Padangusthasana

This pose is done with the help of a long scarf or soft belt. It is an easy way to open up your hip joint, loosen your legs, and strengthen your spine. The second variation also provides a nice abdominal twist and massages the internal organs.

How to do the pose:

+ Lie on your back on the floor and wrap the belt or scarf under the saddle of your foot, grasping the ends in each hand.

+ Straighten and extend the leg up toward the ceiling.

+ Using your arms, start to move your leg around in small circles. Once you feel comfortable with this motion, widen the circles—you can play with this movement to experiment with making the circles bigger or smaller.

+ Be aware of a tendency to arch your back, and keep your spine aligned against the mat. You may have to engage your abdominal muscles to do this.

+ Now bring the circling to a stop and pull your foot toward your head. You will feel a stretch along the back of your leg, so be gentle.

+ Lower your leg to the floor. Take a few breaths, giving yourself a moment to experience how this leg feels compared to the other leg.

+ Tie the scarf or belt around the opposite foot and begin the pose on the other side.

To add a nice spinal twist and stretch the buttocks, try this variation:

+ Grasp both ends of the scarf with the hand that is opposite the raised leg. Let's start with the right leg.

+ Guide your right leg over to your left side.

+ Keep your right arm stretched out on the floor, pointing away from the direction in which you are moving your leg.

+ Keep your head turned, facing your right hand.

+ Hold this for several breaths, enjoying the stretch that is moving from the top of your spine to your foot, and then repeat on the opposite side.

Forward Bend—Paschimottanasana

The forward bend is a wonderful all-around workout. It stretches the body from the top of the head to the soles of the feet, and because of the bending aspect, the abdominal organs also receive a wonderful massage. Take your time with this pose so you can enjoy sinking into the stretch. When you come back to sitting after practicing this posture, your world will feel like a different place.

How to do the pose:

◆ Begin by sitting with your legs extended on the floor, heels pushed away and toes raised, pointing toward your body. Feel your buttocks firm against the floor.

◆ Exhale from your belly. Inhale, raising your arms toward the ceiling and extending your spine out of your hips. Press the crown of your head away from your shoulders.

◆ Exhaling, bend at the waist, keeping your back straight. Your arms will be pointing in front of you. Hold this position for one breath.

◆ On your next exhale, round the back and bring your hands down toward your feet, grasping your calves, ankles, or toes—wherever you can reach.

◆ Bend your elbows toward the floor alongside your knees and bring your head

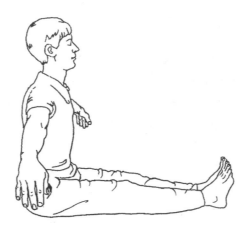

toward your knees, touching your forehead to your knees if possible. Breathe into the stretch.

✦ Hold this position for a few breaths and then raise up on an inhalation, extending your arms with your hands pointed to the ceiling.

◆ Exhale, lowering your arms to your side. Give yourself a few rounds of breathing to sit quietly, your spine straight, feeling the warm glow of this posture.

Head to Knee—Janushirshasana

This is a pose that will remind you to listen to your body if your thoughts begin to wander, as the stretch to the leg can be intense if not done mindfully. It also gives you the opportunity to be aware of the placement of your torso as you extend over the leg, so it helps to build alignment and concentration. It also opens the hips, tones and stimulates the internal organs, and strengthens the spine.

How to do the pose:

◆ Begin sitting on the floor. Extend your legs in front of you. Your back should be straight—allow your abdominal muscles to help hold you up. Breathe easily.

◆ Bend your left leg out to the side, bringing the sole of your left foot up into your right thigh as far as possible. Once you have placed the heel against the inner right thigh, let the left knee drop toward the floor. If you are having trouble doing this, place a folded blanket (about one to two inches high) under your left thigh. Your right foot should be flexed back up toward you.

◆ Inhaling, raise both arms overhead. Feel the lift happening all the way from your buttocks up through your hands. It is easy to let the torso swing out to the left here, pointing over the bent left leg. Be aware of keeping your torso aligned with the extended right leg.

- Pause for a moment in this position and breathe easily. Your arms reach over your head, shoulders relaxed. Both sides of the buttocks are in even contact with the floor, and your torso is open and strong. Bring your attention to your right leg. You are about to bend over it, introducing an enlivening stretch.

- Exhaling, bend forward from your hips. Reach toward your right foot, aiming to interlace the fingers around the toes.

   Note: If reaching your torso over your leg or clasping the extended foot is not possible, try to do the posture with the aid of props. This is simple. Once you have bent your left leg, place your strap around the bottom of your right foot, holding one end of the strap firmly in each hand. Your elbows will be slightly bent. Feel the flex of the foot and the stretch behind the leg. Remain sitting up straight, shoulders down, chest lifted, and hold the pose for several breaths before moving on to the next part of the picture.

- Lower your chest toward your leg. Resist the temptation to drop the head, which would allow you to collapse over the extended leg. Instead, focus on your alignment, taking the time to understand where in your body you experience difficulty. Explore the posture, finding a place of comfort without compromising the position.

- If the stretch behind your right leg is uncomfortable, keep the torso in a position where it doesn't overstretch the back of the leg as you clasp the toes of your extended foot with your hands or your strap.

- Feel the pull along the back of the extended leg. If you can, flex the foot more to increase the stretch.

- Hold the pose for several breaths, then come up and repeat the pose on the other side.

Seal of Union—Yoga Mudra

This is a simple way to find a place of calm within. It tones your abdominal muscles and soothes the central nervous system. The simplicity of the movement gives beginners an opportunity to focus on the breath, so take your time with the inhalations and

> "As an asana is perfected through practice, at a certain stage it becomes spiritual, a mudra. The word mudra means 'a seal, a sealing posture.' The royal houses and nobility use seals to signify their position and authenticity. In ancient times the seal was the confirmation of the sender of a message. The human body is also a seal. We have to discover what is sealed up, what is the secret behind the seal."
> —SWAMI SIVANANDA RADHA

exhalations. Allow yourself to completely fill the belly and lungs with fresh, clean air and to enjoy the sense of emptiness from long, deep exhalations. There are two variations: on the floor and standing. Working with either one of these postures can be a great way to recharge after a hectic day.

How to do the pose:

Variation 1

Kneeling Yoga Mudra

+ Begin the pose kneeling, buttocks back on your heels, hands resting on your knees. If this is uncomfortable, you can place a pillow between the backs of your calves and your buttocks.

+ As you take a deep breath in, lift your hands off your knees and let your arms float back and around behind you.

+ Interlace your fingers, roll your shoulders back and down, straighten your arms, and lengthen the spine by pressing out of the crown of your head.

+ On the next exhalation, bend forward, bringing the chin or forehead to the ground in front of you and raising the hands behind you toward the ceiling.

+ Once you have emptied the lungs and are leaning forward, hold yourself in this position and take several long deep breaths, feeling the massage of the abdominal organs. As you rest in the position, press your arms forward and down toward the floor.

"The ground for compassion is established first by practicing sensitivity toward ourselves. True compassion arises from a healthy sense of self, from an awareness of who we are that honors our own capacities and fears, our own feelings and integrity, along with those of others."

—JACK KORNFIELD

+ Inhaling, return back to your upright seated position. Remain in this position as you exhale, then begin the round again.

+ For a more intense stretch, while in the Forward bend position, roll up onto the top of your head and lift your buttocks up toward the ceiling. Press your arms down toward the floor.

Come out of the posture by resting in the Child's pose.

Variation 2

Standing Yoga Mudra

- Begin in the Mountain pose, taking a few long deep breaths to feel yourself centered in your stance.

- Inhaling, reach behind you with both arms, keeping them straight and extended. Roll your shoulders back and down and open your chest.

- Bring your hands together behind you, interlacing your fingers and straightening your arms. Extend your arms back, as if you are reaching toward something behind you with your clasped hands.

- You may feel a stretch in your shoulders or in your chest—breathe into this and allow your body to relax.

- Exhaling, bend forward, lowering the chin in front of you and raising the hands toward the ceiling. Because you are bending forward, your arms will be stretching forward, toward your head.

- Keep your fingers entwined and pull your shoulder blades toward each other.

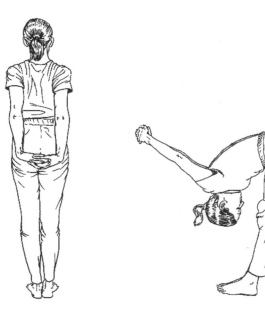

- Once you have emptied the lungs and are leaning forward, hold yourself in this position and take deep breaths for several seconds, feeling the massage of the abdominal organs and the stretch in the back of your legs. Bend your legs at the knees if the stretch is too intense.

- Inhaling, return back to your standing position with your arms extended behind you. Release your hands as you exhale, and bring your arms back to your sides.

- Stand for a minute in the Mountain pose. Allow your breath to be long and rhythmic.

Downward Facing Dog—Adho Mukha Svanasana

The Downward Facing Dog stretches the hamstrings and calf muscles, strengthens the arms, and opens up the chest. A lot of its benefit is dependent on keeping your weight evenly balanced between feet and hands. This way you can lift the buttocks, feeling the movement ripple from the top of your head through your spine and along the backs of your legs. The posture can awaken the pelvic area and tone the abdominal muscles as well

How to do the pose:

- Start in a table position with both palms on the floor directly underneath the shoulders and the knees under the hips. Inhaling, turn your toes under and flex them against the floor.

- Exhaling, push on your hands and toes to raise your hips in the air, forming an inverted V. Position your head so your ears remain between your biceps, extending your spine from the hips to the top of your head.

- Once you have established this position, point your tailbone toward the ceiling, arching your back and pressing your heels into the floor.

- Roll your shoulders out and press your sternum toward the floor.

- Explore the ways in which your weight moves. Where is your center? Are you

Like many poses, the Downward Facing Dog is more than meets the eye. It can appear to be an elaborate toe-touching exercise, but when you actually practice, it becomes an exploration of weight, balance, and focus. This is an example of how practicing yoga differs from simply moving through exercises. The position can be executed by shaping the body into a **V**, but that is not about practicing yoga. When you add the intention to feel the body, to watch the breath and be aware of your thoughts as you shift your weight, exploring and locating your center, then holding the posture becomes a journey of creating union between the mind and body—and possibly the spirit. This makes it yoga.

leaning forward? Be careful not to lean down into your arms. You might think of a string lifting you up toward the ceiling from the base of your spine.

+ Allow your arms to steady you and hold the pose, but not to hold you up. Let your head hang relaxed—even shake it. Bring your belly in toward your navel.

+ Maintain the position for several breaths. To come out of the posture, fold down gently in the Child's pose.

Seated Twist—Ardha Matsyendrasana

The Seated Twist is an all-around torso toner. It massages the abdominal muscles, reduces hip and lower back discomfort, improves the nervous system, and increases spinal elasticity. With regular practice, the posture whittles the waistline, as well. Some say the posture also helps to stimulate kundalini energy.

How to do the pose:

+ Begin by sitting either on the floor or on a folded blanket, legs extended in front of you. Sitting on the blanket helps to take stress off the back and knees.

+ Place both of your palms flat on the floor behind your hips with your fingers pointing behind you.

+ Keeping your left leg extended, bend your right leg and crossing over the left knee, place the right foot on the outside of the extended left leg next to the left knee.

+ Shift your weight onto your right hand and extend your left arm in front of you parallel to the floor, fingers pointing away from your chest.

+ Twist your torso to the right, looking behind you. At the same time, lower your left arm, pressing the elbow against the right knee, resting the left palm on the outside of the extended left knee.

◆ Twist the entire body from the navel area upward, and extend the spine toward the ceiling, looking over your right shoulder. Keep both buttocks on the floor. Take several deep breaths, allowing the spine to twist and massage the abdomen deeply.

To modify this pose, make a change when you lower your raised arm. Instead of hugging your knee with the bent elbow, simply cup your left hand over your right knee, face out to the right, and experience a smaller version of the twist. Again, make sure the movement comes from the belly, not the upper back and neck.

Backward Bends

Back bends not only bend the back—which provides terrific stimulation to the spine and glandular system—but they widen the exposure to the front of the body, an area that is often shielded. Practicing back bends can feel emotional, as they both lift the heart and open it up, allowing laughter, sadness, or a wash of feelings to flood through without any particular rhyme or reason.

Try this mini experience of a back bend: Sit straight in a chair and, inhaling, begin to arch your neck and back. Focus your gaze upward, but don't allow your head to flop back. You may feel an opening in the center of your chest—as if your heart were lifting. You may find yourself laughing. Or perhaps your throat feels tight. Take a moment to relax your face, take in a deep breath, and smile. Your chest and throat are open, your neck is relaxed, and your face is beaming up toward the sun. This is what is possible to feel in all the back-bend postures.

Keep It Safe

To avoid crunching your neck in a back bend, try this simple trick: When leaning your head back, try bringing your lower lip up over your upper lip. If it's difficult, and if you feel a strain in your chin and face, you may be letting your head fall back too far.

Fish Pose—Matsyasana

This pose opens your chest and fills the lungs with air just as a fish opens its gills. It is an energizing posture that strengthens the abdomen, relaxes the throat, and offers a great way to reduce anxiety.

How to do the pose:

+ Lie on your back with your legs extended out in front of you. Keep your legs straight and your feet together.

+ Place your palms under your tailbone, thumbs touching.

+ Inhaling, lift your upper chest and arch your back. Your head will naturally lift and tilt back. Allow the tilt to progress in a careful, gentle manner, taking care to avoid any pressure on your neck.

+ Rest the top of your head lightly against the floor, feeling the expansion of your chest and the strength of your upper back.

+ Bring your hands into a prayer position above your heart. Take three deep breaths, filling your lungs, and letting your exhalation out slowly. This is a new position for the chest, so be mindful of how different it feels to breathe in this position.

+ Hold the position for three breaths. Come out of the pose on an exhalation and pause for a moment to feel your shoulders relax against the mat.

Cobra Pose—Bhujangasana

The Cobra pose strengthens the arms, lower back, and abdominal muscles. It also opens the chest—it actually lifts the heart—and improves posture. It's a great way to prepare the body for more strenuous back bends.

+ Begin by lying on your stomach. Just as you do when starting a standing position, feel the way you are grounded to the floor. Become aware of how it feels to have your chest, stomach, thighs, and knees weighty against the floor. Relax the small of your back. Keep your legs together. Check to see that the tops of your feet are flat against the floor—they should not be flexed. Rest your forehead on the floor.

+ Bend your elbows, placing your hands directly underneath your shoulders. Make sure your elbows remain at your sides throughout the pose. Broaden your chest and roll your shoulder blades back and down. Your shoulders could ride up here, so be aware of keeping them down.

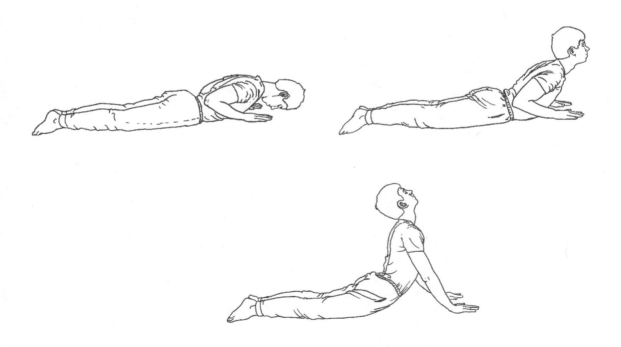

- Place your hands flat on the floor, fingers spread. Keep your gaze a few inches beyond the fingertips.

- Inhaling, lift the head, chest, and shoulders from the floor. Use the strength of the buttocks and lower back muscles to generate and maintain the lift rather than pushing up with the arms. In fact, try lifting your hands off the floor for a moment to make sure you are not relying on your arms.

- Next, press into your hands and use your arms to lift your chest area and your belly as far as the pubic bone. Push the belly button down toward the floor to anchor yourself. The buttocks and legs should be firm but not tense. Press your palms and the tops of your feet into the floor.

- Exhale and hold this position for several breaths. Scan your body for tension, letting the face and throat relax. Bring your attention to the expansion in your chest and heart area. Press out of the crown of your head and lengthen the spine.

- Come out of the pose slowly, feeling the spine adjust back to its normal curvature. Rest for a moment on the floor or in the Child's pose.

Bow Pose—Dhanurasana

The Bow pose brings the gifts of strength and elasticity to your entire back while stretching the chest, shoulders, abdominal muscles, and thighs. It tones the inner organs and stimulates the kidneys and adrenals. And since it requires focus to do well, it also helps to hone your concentration.

Though it is a beginner's pose, it isn't simple, so be mindful of any strain as you hold the position. Find a place where you can experience the pose without forcing it, exploring your ability to relax into yourself in the face of a challenge. When you're finished, slide easily into the Child's pose for several breaths.

How to do the pose:

- Prepare for the pose by lying facedown on the floor with your arms resting alongside your body. Palms will be against the floor.

- Bend your legs up behind you until the shinbones are vertical—think about the way some children lie on their bellies, watching their favorite TV show with their legs bent up in the air—and bring your feet together so they move as one. Reach back with your hands and grasp your ankles.

+ Inhaling, lift your upper body (as you did in the Cobra pose) from the floor as far as you can.

+ Exhaling, move your feet straight up toward the ceiling, just an inch or so. You will feel the pubic bone pressing against the floor. If this is uncomfortable, place a blanket underneath you. Continue to inch your feet up breath by breath, finding a place where you are discovering new movement but are not pushing into a feeling of discomfort. Listen to your body.

+ Release the pose.

+ Now that you have prepared yourself for the pose, continue into actually becoming a bow. Clasp your ankles, and as you inhale, lift your chest up off the floor.

+ Exhaling, lift your legs up toward the ceiling. Your feet will be about one foot apart, and your body will begin to arch back, like a bow. The arms should be straight. Do not rock here. Instead, using the breath, continue to stretch up through the torso.

+ Be aware of where your lifting action is coming from. Allow it to emanate from the legs and spine, not from the arms. When you have found a place of comfort, lift your head so you are looking toward the ceiling. Feel the energy coursing from the top of your head through your spine and up to the soles of your feet, as if it is illuminating the shape of the bow.

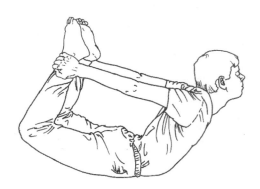

+ You might want to take a moment to direct the breath toward the heart, even if just for one inhalation. Use the open sensation of the posture to send your heart a message.

Variation

Clasp your right ankle with your right arm and extend your left leg back, flat on the floor. Reach your left arm out in front of you. Keep your focus on balance, being mindful not to lean over to the side that is straight. This is a great exercise for exploring steadiness and endurance.

Bridge Pose—Sethu Bandhasana

Here's an opportunity not only to build a bridge but to build up your listening muscles, as well. The Bridge is useful for strengthening the spine and stimulates the pituitary, thyroid, and adrenal glands. But it is also a pose that takes time and awareness, as it is a challenging back-bending position. To get the most from this pose, move into it slowly, and with care. The Cobra is a good pose to do to prepare for the Bridge.

How to do the pose:

+ Lie flat on the floor on your back. Bend your legs at the knees, keeping your feet a little more than hip-distance apart. Point your toes forward, and let your arms lay comfortably along your sides, palms flat on the floor.
+ Inhaling, lift your hips up toward the ceiling. You may need to pull your feet in toward you to help hoist the hips.

> "If the mind is happy, not only the body but the whole world will be happy. So you must find out how to become happy yourself. Wanting to reform the world without discovering your true self is like trying to cover the whole world with leather to avoid the pain of walking on stones and thorns. It is much simpler to wear shoes."
> —RAMANA MAHARSHI

+ Exhaling, lift the hips higher. Your head, neck, and shoulders remain on the floor. Keep your arms flat on the floor next to your body, palms on the ground or hands clasping your ankles.

+ Your body is now forming an arc. Keep the buttocks firm and the knees in line with the ankles—make sure the knees do not flop open. Maintain this position for several breaths.

+ Once you are comfortable with the Bridge, it is a pleasure to "ride" the posture. Until then, watch for any pinching in the back or around the neck area, and move out of the posture if you feel these sensations.

Variation

Clasp the hands under the back. This will increase your arch. Pull your shoulder blades together, expanding your chest.

Come down slowly and bring your knees to your chest to release any tension in the lower back.

Camel Pose—Ustrasana

The Camel pose opens the shoulders and chest, so it's great for people who sit at a keyboard all day. It increases the lung capacity, stretches the abdomen, and can help to relieve the discomfort of sciatica. It stretches the thighs, as well. The stretch will be enhanced by imagining you are pressing your thighs against a wall in front of you.

Because the camel activates and opens up the area around the heart and throat, you may feel emotions after just a few moments in this position. You might feel sadness or a feeling of being choked up, as if you needed to cry. This is natural for any posture that stimulates this area. If it happens as you practice the Camel, draw on your tools of awareness and acceptance—and bring the teachings of Bahkti yoga to your heart center.

How to do the pose:

+ Get into a kneeling position, the knees about hip width apart and feet almost touching. Your feet will be top-down against the floor, not flexed.

+ Place your hands on your lower back, tighten the thigh and buttocks muscles and arch back.

+ Next, lower your arms and the top of your body back, reaching toward your heels. If you can rest your hands on your heels, do so. Press your hips forward as if you were pressing against a wall. If this is too difficult, you can

place a few pillows on top of your feet so you can easily rest your hands on this elevated platform.

+ If your usual posture is such that your shoulders are slightly hunched, this movement will introduce a very different feeling. Allow yourself to breathe into the stretch, even if it feels unfamiliar.

+ Hold this position for several breaths. You may notice a lift in the back and shoulder blade area when you first come out of the pose. See if you can maintain this lift for a few moments through awareness and intention.

Regular practice of the Camel pose will teach the shoulders to square and the chest to lift, creating a prouder, more confident carriage. Play with this experience on your own. Walk around after practicing the pose, allowing its stretch to become an easy sense of openness in your upper body, and sense how it might feel to present yourself to the world with this posture.

Keep it Safe

The Camel and Rabbit poses can both provide intense stretches, so save these poses for the end of your practice when your body is warmed up.

Rabbit Pose—Sasangasana

The Rabbit pose offers a wonderful repose to the Camel and other back bends, as it provides a maximum longitudinal extension to the spine. It stretches the spine, creating flexibility and elasticity. If you work at a computer, the shoulder and upper back stretch is a wonderful way to let tension roll away. The Rabbit also improves digestion and helps with sinus problems.

How to do the pose:

- Begin in the kneeling position, your buttocks resting on your heels, your spine straight. Breathe easily, centering yourself.

- Reach your arms around and clasp your heels. Your thumb should be on the outside so you are cradling your heels in your palms.

- Exhaling, curl forward, lowering your chin to your chest. Touch your forehead to your knees and let the top of your head graze the floor. Take care to not let your weight fall forward onto the top of your head.

- Lift your hips, rolling your body forward until your arms are straight and your thighs are perpendicular to the floor. Support your weight with the tension between your arms and heels.

- Inch your knees forward toward the forehead. One goal of the posture is to have the forehead touching the knees, but this may take practice. When the forehead and knees are distant, the back needs to stretch out, become supple, and relax. Time and practice will let this happen.

- To come out of the pose, sit up slowly and direct the breath into the new expanse in your upper back.

Hero Pose—Virasana

The Hero sits tall and proud. The Hero is also very wise and knows when to listen to the body and to take things slowly. This pose refreshes the legs and stretches the thighs and buttocks.

How to do the pose:

- Sit on the floor with your legs extended.

- Fold both legs, placing one knee directly on top of the other.

- Lift and extend the spine, pressing out of the crown of your head. Roll your shoulders back and down.

- Place hands on soles of feet.

- Feel the stretch in the thighs and buttocks muscles.

- Take several long deep breaths, then reverse the leg that is on top.

Inversions

Here's a chance to benefit from having your life turned upside down. Inversions are challenging, enlivening, and terrific for the body. The reverse in gravity relieves pressure on the abdominal organs, stimulates the glandular system, and enhances circulation to the chest and head.

Inversions leave the body and mind feeling exhilarated and rested. Once you're comfortable looking toward the ceiling (instead of the floor) in order to see your feet, inversions will become an important part of your practice.

Proceed slowly, however, as many of the postures can lead to neck and back strain if not done properly. Inversion poses require you to listen to your body, responding to its messages to pause, slow down, or stop. Because they take concentration—especially when you are first starting out—inversions can deepen the connection between mind and body. You may want to ask your yoga instructor to guide you through these before trying them on your own.

Keep It Safe

All inverted postures should be avoided under certain circumstances. If you have high blood pressure, heart problems, or are pregnant, do not attempt inversions without first checking with your doctor.

Half Shoulder Stand—Ardha Sarvangasana

Welcome to the magic of gravity! This inversion stimulates the thyroid gland and tones your internal organs. It is also restful for the heart, as it doesn't have to pump as hard to the extremities when inverted. Some folks also find it helps with headaches. Once you are comfortable with this posture it may become effortless, offering you a familiar place to simply hang out, letting all the worries of the day float away while you reenergize your body.

How to do the pose:

+ Lie flat on your back on the floor. Since you're about to turn your world upside down, take just a moment to check in with yourself. Can you feel your shoulder blades, the small of your back, your heels? Is your breath even and rhythmic?

+ Bring your knees over your chest. This gives the small of your back a nice stretch and massages your internal organs.

+ Put your arms on the floor, palms down. Let your arms lengthen away from the shoulders.

+ Move your hands to your lower back, where they will help to support you. Face your fingers inward.

+ Exhaling, lift your legs up. Contract your abdominal muscles to assist in the lift—do not just swing the legs up.

+ Extend your legs toward the ceiling, allowing your elbows and hands to take the weight of your body.

+ Remain inverted for several breaths. To come out of the pose, fold your knees back against your chest and roll slowly back to sitting.

+ Spend a moment sitting quietly after the inversion, allowing yourself to come to center.

Full Shoulder Stand—Sarvangasana

+ Return to the inverted position of the Half Shoulder Stand.

+ Move your hands from the small of your back toward your shoulder blades.

+ Straighten your legs up toward the ceiling. The trick to raising them up and straight is to think up, up, up through your feet. Keep the calves and feet relaxed, though. Check to make sure this is happening by wiggling your toes.

+ Keep your legs quiet by focusing on your belly and thighs. Lift from your torso. Keep your spine straight—even in this position, your buttocks can swing back and forth. Take a moment to make sure you are aligned.

+ Keep your hands cupped against your back. Unlike the Half Shoulder Stand, your arms are critical to this posture. The elbows should stay parallel, because if they splay out you may lose the foundation of the stand.

+ Though your hands are assisting you, be careful not to let your weight collapse into them. Hold your legs up through the abdominal muscles. Explore the way in which you are holding your weight by dropping your arms back to your sides. Your legs should stay in the pose as if your hands were still at the small of your back.

+ To come out of the pose, roll down gently, vertebra by vertebra. As with the Half Shoulder Stand, allow yourself time to sit in stillness after the inversion.

Caution: Come out of the position if you feel pinching in the neck or pressure in the head, ears, eyes, or throat. Practice the Half Shoulder Stand until you feel strong enough to move into the Full Shoulder Stand.

Plough—Halasana

The Plough is a relaxing, passive position. It stimulates the spine, strengthens the nervous system, and tones the internal organs. It offers an intense neck and lower back stretch, as well, so if your neck is stiff, approach this pose gradually.

How to do the pose:

+ Lie on your back, bend your knees, and place your hands on the floor.

+ Inhaling, press your hands into the floor, raise your legs, hips, and buttocks off the floor by rolling backward as if you were about to try doing a backward somersault—keeping your legs bent.

+ Exhaling, straighten your legs and lower your feet toward the floor behind you. If you cannot touch your toes to the floor, do not force it. Instead, remain with your legs suspended. As you breathe into the stretch, the shoulders and small of the back will release and your feet may drop closer to the floor, but the posture is beneficial in either position.

+ You can press your hands against the small of your back, you can allow the arms to rest against the floor, palms down, or you can straighten the arms on the floor, interlace your fingers, and pull your shoulder blades together.

+ Hold this pose for several breaths. Scan your spine with your mind, tracing it from the top of your head to your lower back. Take notice of the spots that are loosening, and direct your breath to the places where tension is hanging on. Keep the weight on your shoulders, not your neck and head.

+ To come out of the pose, roll back slowly, taking a moment to notice the softening and lengthening in your spine.

Headstand—Sirsasana

The Headstand can be an absolute pleasure. It stimulates the entire system, improving circulation and strengthening the nervous system. The benefits of the posture come most easily when the body is prepared, as it is a strenuous posture. Start out against a wall so you can use it to support your legs. Make sure you bring sufficient arm, shoulder, neck, and stomach strength to the Headstand.

How to do the pose:

- Start from your hands and knees, facing the wall.

- Interlace your fingers, and rest your forearms and hands with your elbows about a forearm apart. You are establishing the foundation for your Headstand at this point.

- Lower your head down into your cupped hands, resting the top of your head on the floor. Pressing down on your forearms, raise your buttocks slightly and begin to walk your feet toward your body. You will begin to sense the strength in your arms. If your arms tremble, this may be as far as you want to go without instruction. You do not want to place undue pressure on your head and neck.

"Strength that has effort in it is not what you need; you need
the strength that is the result of ease."

—IDA ROLF

+ Keep your legs bent until your torso is perpendicular to the floor. At this point it may help your balance to rest your feet against the wall.

+ Slowly raise your feet in the air. You may be tempted to kick your legs up, but do not do so. Instead, walk your feet slowly up the wall, taking small, careful steps until your legs rest against the wall. Focus on your base: arms, elbows, head, shoulders, and belly. Feel their energy and strength, as they are now holding you up. Keep your legs still.

+ Allow yourself to stay here for several breaths. For beginners, the goal is to maintain the position in a quiet, centered space. Once that has been achieved, bringing deep-breathing exercises to the Headstand will follow.

+ To come down, bend your legs and lower them slowly to the floor and come back to your knees.

Rest in the Child's pose.

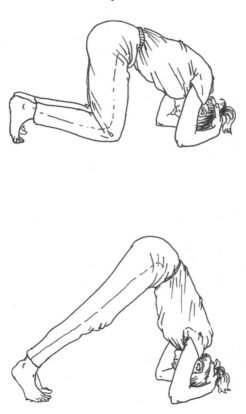

One pose that can help you to prepare for the Headstand is the Mountain pose, as the lessons of balance that the Mountain pose teaches will help you stay steady when you are upside down. Your weight must be supported by your arms, shoulders, and the strength of your abdomen, as pressure on the top of your head will lead to injury. Develop a deep understanding of balance and a sensitivity to weight distribution by standing upright before bringing yourself to the Headstand.

ENDING THE PRACTICE

Cross-legged Posture—Sukhasana

The meaning of this posture's Sanskrit name describes the feeling it offers. *Sukha* means "joy," "pleasure," or "ease," and this is the easiest of all the seated poses. It is also called the Easy Seated pose or the Tailor's pose.

Though it may appear to be no more than just sitting cross-legged on the floor, its practice actually entails a surprising level of attention and sensitivity. The posture may reveal areas of tightness and weakness, especially in the lower back, hips, and thighs.

The pose facilitates breathing, quiets the mind, and creates a feeling of stillness throughout the body.

How to do the pose:

- Sit on the floor with legs crossed, keeping your feet away from the buttocks and the lower legs crossed between the ankles and shins.

- You may want to sit on the edge of a folded blanket if your back is rounding or sinking, or if your knees lift up above the line of the pelvis.

- To enhance the challenge of this pose, try to sit with the leg that is less comfortable on top. This will help to balance your body.

- Straighten your back, lifting from the lower back, and pull your shoulders back and down.

- Open your chest, lengthen your neck, and keep the chin posed parallel to the floor.

- Rest your hands on your knees, palms facedown, and breathe.

Lotus—Padmasana

The Lotus pose represents a lotus flower open to the light. It's a pose most beginners have heard about and are eager to do, but because of the pressure it may bring to your knees, ankles, or hip joints, be careful—go into it with care.

Also, even if you can achieve the pose, don't maintain it if you feel discomfort. The goal of the Lotus pose is to provide a quiet posture for meditation, so if you are counting the seconds until your knees can be freed, the point of the pose will be lost. If the full Lotus is uncomfortable, use the Cross-legged posture. They both support the meditation process.

How to do the pose:

- Sit on the floor, breathing deeply.

- Place your left ankle on top of your right thigh, then carefully lift your right ankle and place it on your left thigh. Switch sides whenever you practice.

- Sit comfortably, enjoying the stable foundation you have built for yourself.

Corpse Pose—Savasana

Of all the gifts yoga offers, the emphasis on relaxation may be its most beneficial. This is because it is often more of a challenge for people to lie prone on the floor than to stand on one leg. For some, it is more difficult to relax than to struggle. And of all the new experiences your body may encounter during a yoga practice, deep relaxation may be the most unfamiliar.

Like balance, flexibility, and strength, relaxation is a tool to be used off the mat. Many of us are so absorbed with getting things done and moving quickly that to simply relax seems out of the question—when in fact it is exactly the answer we need. Allowing the body to sink into a peaceful, calm state is the way we can begin to introduce a serene and quiet mind as everyday sensations.

But the Corpse is much more than a stress-reduction tool. The Corpse pose is a way of providing appropriate closure for yoga practice. It is not just a nap tacked onto the end of a workout, not by any means. Taking the time to experience stillness, letting the blood flow normally again, respecting the fact that it takes time for the shifts in energy, the sensations in the body, and the thoughts of the mind to sort themselves out is of deep importance. It is a way of honoring your efforts and the practice itself.

In addition, although the posture may appear to be easy, relaxing fully is actually quite challenging. One does not master deep relaxation in the Corpse pose simply by lying still.

How to do the pose:

+ Lie on your back, eyes closed, legs outstretched, about two to three feet apart. Let your toes fall out to the sides.

+ Separate your arms, palms facing up. Release the tension in your neck by rolling your head side to side, and roll your shoulders down away from your ears.

- Breathing naturally, scan your body, pausing when you sense fatigue, tension, or stress. Breathe more deeply, directing the breath to these areas.

- Once you have taken a long, quiet journey through your body, bring your attention to your breath. Allow any residual tension to be released as you deepen the breath.

- Return to normal breathing. Watch your inhalations and exhalations, focusing only on the sound of your breath. As your mind wanders, trying to remember where you parked the car, hoping someone at the office has finished a project, replaying a debate you're having with a family member, just let these thoughts go. Return to the breath, focusing on the sound it makes, its rhythm, the way it fills your lungs and belly. Whenever your thoughts arise, watch them rise up in your mind, acknowledge them, and send them drifting away with your exhalation.

Practice this for at least five minutes.

Come out of the Corpse pose slowly. Wiggle your fingers and toes. Move your awareness to the room, recalling where you are. Concentrate on keeping the mind quiet as you come out of the Corpse and complete your routine.

Bend your knees, roll over on your side, and pause in the Child pose. Bring yourself to a seated position. There is no hurry. Sit there, savoring the experience before you come to standing and move into the rest of your day.

 If you have an exaggerated lumbar curve (or, as you may have heard it called, a swayback), you may find that placing a pillow or a bolster under the back of your knees helps your back to relax more. Some beginners find that propping the feet up on a padded chair helps their back to relax into the floor. Try placing an eye bag over your eyes to deepen the practice.

"God wants nothing from you but the gift of a peaceful heart."
—MEISTER ECKHART

SUGGESTED READING

Christensen, Alice. *20-Minute Yoga Workouts.* New York: Fawcett, 1995.

Myers, Esther. *Yoga and You: Energizing and Relaxing Yoga for New and Experienced Students.* Boston: Shambhala, 1997.

SUGGESTED AUDIOTAPES

Alan Watts Teaches Meditation. Alan Watts. Audio Renaissance, 1992.

The Art of Relaxation: A Collection of Irresistible Soothing Music. Relaxation Co., 1996.

Awakening Compassion: Meditation Practice for Difficult Times. Pema Chodron. Sounds True, 1997.

Beginner's Guide to Meditation. Joan Borysenko. Hay House, 1998.

Being Peace. Thich Nhat Hanh. 1995.

Break Through Difficult Emotions: How to Transform Painful Feelings with Mindfulness Meditation. Shinzen Young. Sounds True, 1997.

Conscious Breathing: Breathwork for Health, Stress Release, and Personal Mastery. Gay Hendricks. AudioSource.

Five Classic Meditations: Mantra, Vipassana, Karma Yoga, Loving Kindness, Kabbalah. Shinzen Young. Audio Renaissance, 1990.

The Heart of Spiritual Practice. Jack Kornfield. 1997.

The Heart of Understanding. Thich Nhat Hanh. 1995.

Meditation for Beginners. Jack Kornfield. 1998.

101 Ways to Transform Your Life. Wayne W. Dyer. Hay House Audio, 1998.

Sutras. Donovan. 1996.

Yoga at the Edge: Advancing Your Practice. Todd Norian.

Yoga Music of the Heart. Wai Lana and Siddha. 1998.

Yoga Zone: Music for Meditation. Various artists. BMG/Windham Hill, 1998.

Yoga Zone: Music for Yoga Practice. Various artists. BMG/Windham Hill, 1998.

SUGGESTED VIDEOS

Basic Yoga. Alice Christensen, American Yoga Association. Can be ordered from American Yoga Association, 513 South Orange Avenue, Sarasota, FL 34326.

The Homestretch—Yoga in Five Easy Pieces. Patricia Duffy. To order, call 1-206-364-7019.

Lilias! Alive with Yoga. Lilias Folan. Can be ordered from Body Trends at 1-800-549-1667 or P.O. Box 3588, Santa Barbara, CA 93130.

New Yoga Basics. Kathy Smith.

Yoga Basics. Lilias Folan.

Yoga Journal's Yoga Practice (the set of the six tapes in *Yoga Journal*'s yoga practice series). 1996. All *Yoga Journal* videos can be ordered from Living Arts, P.O. Box 2939, Dept. YJ406, Venice, CA 90291.

Yoga Journal's Yoga Practice for Beginners. Patricia Walden.

Yoga Journal's Yoga Practice for Energy. Rodney Yee.

Yoga Journal's Yoga Practice for Flexibility. Patricia Walden.

Yoga Journal's Yoga Practice for Meditation. Rodney Yee.

Yoga Journal's Yoga Practice for Relaxation. Patricia Walden and Rodney Yee.

Yoga Journal's Yoga Practice for Strength. Rodney Yee.

Yoga Zone Conditioning and Stress Release. Alan Finger.

9.

Suggested Routines

You can create your own yoga practice according to the time of day, how you are feel-ing, or the amount of time you have. Here are a number of routines that will fit al-most any circumstance or schedule. They are designed to provide suggestions for real-life scenarios—such as yoga on the road or to use in times of emotional stress.

Wake-up Routines

These are great ways to start the day—whether you have just a few minutes or can schedule more time.

Ten Minutes

Victorious Breath (p. 76)

Knee Down Twist (p. 96)

Leg Assisted Tie (p. 118)

Child's Pose (p. 116)

Neck Rolls (p. 84)

Forearm Stretch (p. 88)

Seal of Union (p. 123)

Twenty-five Minutes

Victorious Breath (p. 76)

Knee Down Twist (p. 96)

Knee to Chest Pose (p. 94)

Leg Assisted Tie (p. 118)

Child's Pose (p. 116)

Neck Rolls (p. 84)

Forearm Stretch (p. 88)

Seal of Union (p. 123)

Cobra Pose (p. 132)

Head to Knee (p. 122)

Workplace Pause and Refresher

Here's an easy way to bring yoga into your office—or wherever you might need a mid-day refresher.

Swinging Twist (p. 101)

Shoulder Stretch (p. 106)

Standing Yoga Mudra (p. 126)

Neck Rolls (p. 84)

Victorious Breath (p. 76)

Eye Calisthenics (p. 25)

Unwinding Sequence

These routines provide a calming, restful practice at the end of the day.

Ten Minutes

Mountain Pose (p. 99)

Half Moon Pose (p. 102)

Swinging Twist (p. 101)

Downward Facing Dog (p. 127)

Neck Rolls (p. 84)

Cobra Pose (p. 132)

Bow Pose (p. 133)

Seal of Union (p. 123)

Camel Pose (p. 137)

Head to Knee (p. 122)

Corpse Pose (p. 149)

Jet-lag Tune-up

Here's a way to take yoga on the road. If you are feeling weary when you get to your hotel room, take about twenty minutes to practice this sequence. It is designed to counteract the effect of a long flight or drive, jet lag, eating on the run, and other stresses of travel.

Standing Poses

Mountain Pose (p. 99)

Half Moon Pose (p. 102)

Swinging Twist (p. 101)

Standing Yoga Mudra (p. 126)

Standing Head to Knee (p. 112)

Downward Facing Dog (p. 127)

Tree Pose (p. 104)

Floor Poses

Neck Rolls (p. 84)

Cat and Dog Stretch (p. 86)

Head to Knee (p. 122)

Knee Down Twist (p. 96)

Child's Pose (p. 116)

Kneeling Yoga Mudra (p. 124)

Leg Assisted Tie (p. 118)

Knee to Chest Pose (p. 94)

Emotional Clearing

Do you ever feel like your emotions are taking over your mind, leaving you without the perspective and clarity you need? This sequence is both rejuvenating and restful, so you can get rid of your "mental knots" and get a clearer view of what's going on in your life.

Child's Pose (p. 116)

Knee to Chest Pose (p. 94)

Om Breath (p. 78)

Meditation (p. 179)

Corpse Pose (p. 149)

Flu Fighter

Here's something we can all relate to: waking up to the aches and pains of the common cold or flu. This routine is almost as good as Mom's chicken noodle soup for helping the body fight the sore throat, stuffiness, and general tired feeling of the common cold.

Cobra Pose (p. 132)

Camel Pose (p. 137)

Bridge Pose (p. 135)

Child's Pose (p. 116)

Rabbit Pose (p. 138)

Half Shoulder Stand (p. 141)

Plough (p. 143)

Forward Bend (p. 120)

Recharge!

Say you've had a long day, and by early evening you're ready to pack it in—but you can't. You have a social or professional event that you are obligated to attend. This sequence will recharge your batteries so you can put the day behind you and go into the evening feeling refreshed and balanced.

Salutation to the Sun (p. 90)

Standing Head to Knee (p. 112)

Triangle Pose (p. 107)

Warrior Pose (p. 190)

Balancing Stick Pose (p. 111)

Tree Pose (p. 104)

Peaceful Self-Loving

This routine is for the times when you need to be alone, nurturing yourself with an extra ounce of self-love. It may be a time when you need to soothe troubles or to pamper a tired spirit.

Child's Pose (p. 116)

Cobra Pose (p. 132)

Seal of Union (p. 123)

Bow Pose (p. 133)

Camel Pose (p. 137)

Bridge Pose (p. 135)

Half Shoulder Stand (p. 141)

Plough (p. 143)

Fish Pose (p. 131)

Seated Twist (p. 129)

Forward Bend (p. 120)

Hero Pose (p. 140)

Victorious Breath (p. 76)

Alternate Nostril Breathing (p. 81)

Corpse Pose (p. 149)

Yoga in Community

10

If you are in a yoga class as a beginner, you may wonder why people who have been studying for years also attend classes—can't they do this at home by now? You may also wonder what the point is of going to a class at all, especially if you have an expert teacher at home, on videotape.

These are excellent points, and all reasons to think about what a class can offer you.

Many beginners report that being in a class helps ease the initial jitters. For example, when the teacher is modeling the Triangle pose to the right, and you realize you're bending to the left, look around the room. You'll see people going every which way, so you can laugh at yourself and relax into feeling that you are not alone. Learning yoga in a class can help you to accept yourself, as once you see that everybody has the same struggles, the whole idea of doing it right or wrong can be diffused.

Some folks think that belonging to a class is an important part of the yoga practice because being in community can teach you something you cannot learn in solitude. Hank Gerson spoke about rediscovering this after a five-day retreat at Omega Institute with teachers from the Yoga Zone.

"I have been studying yoga for a while, but I always had a hermetic practice,"

"In the West we tend to see the body as separate from the psyche, representing an independent part of nature that must be curbed and kept subservient to our wishes. Whether conscious or unconscious, this is the paradigm we've inherited. And yet, the fullest sense of the words 'to balance' can mean to merge with the environment and other people. Ultimately, our practice of yoga need no longer seem separate from the life processes around us."

—DONNA FARHI

he explained. "I would always practice alone, which I liked, but I thought I may have been missing something. That's why I decided to come to the class. I discovered that what I was missing is what I would call friendship yoga."

This idea of "friendship yoga" offered Gerson insights that he may not have had—or been aware of having—if he was on his own. "Being in the class has enabled

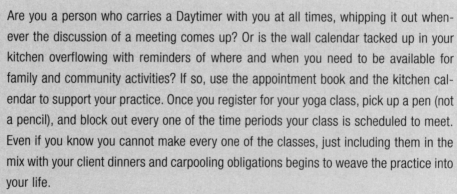

Are you a person who carries a Daytimer with you at all times, whipping it out whenever the discussion of a meeting comes up? Or is the wall calendar tacked up in your kitchen overflowing with reminders of where and when you need to be available for family and community activities? If so, use the appointment book and the kitchen calendar to support your practice. Once you register for your yoga class, pick up a pen (not a pencil), and block out every one of the time periods your class is scheduled to meet. Even if you know you cannot make every one of the classes, just including them in the mix with your client dinners and carpooling obligations begins to weave the practice into your life.

If you are called away on a last-minute business trip and you see the class inked into your book as you make travel plans, this is a perfect opportunity to incorporate flexibility into your life. Just because you cannot be in the classroom doesn't mean you need to cancel your appointment with yoga. Plan to practice in your hotel room when you would have been taking the class. It may turn out to be a great opportunity to learn more about how the practice feels when you do it outside of the classroom.

"No matter what you are doing, keep the undercurrent of happiness. Learn to be secretly happy within your heart despite all circumstances."

—PARAMAHANSA YOGANANDA

me to articulate what is going on inside me," he said. "Being in community with yoga is a way of being in union. This connection makes me more aware and more sensitive, and it feels better. It adds an element of fun."

Friendship yoga can also mean signing up for a class with a friend. Why not share this great experience? Joining a yoga class with a buddy can add a new dimension to your friendship and offer support to your practice.

Being in a class can also offer resources, especially for a novice. If your curiosity is sparked by trying a healthier diet, for example, you will probably generate a lot of conversation if you mention this in the coatroom after class. You will also probably find plenty of people who want to share their experiences if you wonder aloud about whether yoga can reduce the stress in your life.

Another plus about joining a class is its regularity. Knowing that you have a specific evening set aside each week is a way of maintaining your practice and of taking care of yourself.

And though yoga can be learned from books and tapes, the guidance of a teacher is invaluable, especially as you begin your practice. A teacher can observe your posture from all angles, offering suggestions for minor adjustments as you explore each pose. This will help you to learn the postures correctly from the beginning, which means the practice you develop on your own will be more satisfying in the long run.

Here are some things to keep in mind when you are looking for a class:

+ Shop around. Check out the bulletin board in your health food store or fitness center for announcements of classes. There are also free newspapers in most major cities that list a plethora of health-related activities, and these are usually available at the natural food store or library.

+ Ask around. It is perfectly okay to request references when you call or visit a yoga studio.

"Never place a period where God has placed a comma."
—GRACIE ALLEN

- Go to the source. Another way to find a teacher, especially if you know what style you are interested in, is to call the main center for that style and ask for teachers in your area. If you are interested in Integral yoga, for example, you can call their center in Virginia and ask for a local teacher. The centers are listed at the end of Chapter 3.

- Make sure you connect with the teacher. As discussed earlier, different teachers offer different styles. Ask if you can observe a class before you register.

- Check out the deals. Many studios offer free sessions at the beginning of a semester, so you can try a few classes before you decide. Most also let you visit classes other than your own if you have missed yours—so you can make it up—and offer a discount depending on the number of sessions you sign up for.

- Get a feel for the group. If the teacher bases the class on a particular school, such as Kripalu, Integral yoga, or Ashtanga yoga, the spirit of the group may reflect this.

- Do you want to be a little fish in a big pond? Think about the size of the class you want. Classes taught in a yoga center or studio may have ten or more students. This can be a good choice if you want personal attention but also want to blend into the crowd.

- Or do you want to be a big fish in a little pond? If you want more individualized attention, however, you may want to look for someone who teaches out of his or her own home. Many yoga teachers convert an extra room into a teaching space, clearing it out to make room for sticky mats and stacking blankets in the corner for restorative poses or deep relaxation. In this case, you may get a great deal of attention, and the group may be more intimate than a class in a center or spa. When you call people who teach out of their own home, make sure you contact references.

+ Do your homework. When practicing on your own, remember back to the
  points your teacher made when you did the same poses in class and integrate
  them into your own practice.

Participating in a class is also about being part of something. It is about opening
yourself up to joining an ad hoc team, all thrown together to learn about being
healthier and more present to your lives. Though you are all in the class for different
reasons, at some level you're really in it together. Take advantage of the fellowship you
can find in a yoga class. You will unroll your mats as strangers but will chant your final "om" as friends.

Off the Mat, Into Community

The lessons of yoga that can be taken off the mat and into your own life may reveal themselves in the way you interact with others. This is because the ideas of union and con-

> "If you want others to be happy, practice compassion.
> If you want to be happy, practice compassion."
> —HIS HOLINESS THE DALAI LAMA

nection that are inherent to yoga are not experienced only between the self and the Divine, nor are they limited to the way one experiences the inner self. The connection that yoga teaches is about relationships and community, as well—from intimate connections and family to friends, colleagues, and the greater community of all living things.

These lessons usually will be experienced as part of your own inner awakening before you are able to bring them to your relationships with others. Flexibility, for example, is a vital part of maintaining healthy relationships, but it is difficult to be flexible with others—especially with their demands—if you don't know how to bend around your own needs first.

Many students of yoga experience a more flexible attitude in general once they develop a practice. As they feel their bodies move with more ease, they find a flow in the way they approach problems or a more relaxed attitude. Once this overall sense of bending and stretching is incorporated into one's own life, it will start to shift into the way relationships are experienced, as well—because the way we experience relationships is really an extension of ourselves.

This is possible for balance, too. How can a relationship have the give and take it needs for balance if the people involved don't have a clear sense of their internal balance, separate from the relationship? Once you learn to live in a way that feels balanced in the day to day, creating an equal relationship is simply an expression of that part of yourself. And for many students of yoga, finding their own inner balance is a process that starts on the mat.

The same can be said for alignment, strength, and endurance. These are all areas that are nurtured and developed through yoga practice, brought into daily life little by little, and may begin to appear as elements of relationship and community.

Though each of these aspects contributes to healthier, more satisfying relationships, the lessons of yoga that are most profound for relationships and pertinent for living in community have to do with listening and being present.

"The higher goal of spiritual living is not to amass a wealth of
information, but to face sacred moments."

—RABBI ABRAHAM HERSCHEL

Have you experienced the rejuvenating spirit of yoga? It can be found in the moment when your inner voice is heard or when the restful feeling that follows your practice seeps deep within you, softening your whole being. These experiences are one way of feeling connection with the Divine. They are a sure way of hearing what your true inner self is saying, and they can be reminders of the joy and sweetness of being alive. These are also the kinds of experiences that you can have with others.

It is important to remember that you have these moments in part because of yoga and in part because of your readiness to have them. Remembering this means that you can be willing to have this level of connection whether you are alone in meditation or with your spouse and kids, waiting in line for the movies.

Once you experience the deep listening and feeling of oneness in yoga, you know that it is possible—in fact, that it is probable—to evoke it in every area of your life. To have the belief that your life can feel this rewarding, this authentic, and this full of grace on a day-to-day basis is what allows yoga to come alive in your relationships and in community.

The connection doesn't stop just with you and your community or friendships. Once you let your light shine, others will be reminded of their own possibilities, which they will then spread through their own light. At the same time, what you generate by being present in your connection with others—integrity, laughter, respect, creativity, and love—you also nurture within yourself.

It's really quite simple: When you begin to practice yoga, you may start to feel really good. As you deepen your practice and watch the way this goodness permeates

"Three things in human life are important: The first is to be kind.
The second is to be kind. The third is to be kind."

—WILLIAM JAMES

> "By inviting the sacred into our hearts and into our most intimate relationships, we are able to actively transform our lives and align them more and more with the great universal ideals of yoga. . . . When we truly love, we are in harmony not only with our beloved but with all living things. Love is blind, insofar as it makes no distinctions but extends to everyone and everything.
>
> "When we love someone, we may well like her beauty and character, or his good looks and wit. However, what we love, if we truly love, cannot be catalogued in this fashion, because it concerns a person's indefinable essence. Since that essence is the same in all of us, genuine love is unqualified. So, love also includes the desire to merge completely, which is indeed the condition of our spiritual essence, the transcendental Self (atman). At the highest level of existence, we are all united."
>
> —GEORG FEUERSTEIN, STEPHAN BODIAN, WITH THE STAFF OF
> *YOGA JOURNAL, LIVING YOGA*

your life, it may seem like the wisest choice to generate the feeling wherever you go. Why not? Once you start to feel good, why create anything else?

As you bring this inner knowing to your relationships and community, the quality of your interactions will most likely change. They will reflect the same sense of peace, rejuvenation, and energy that you initially experienced on your own, on the mat. The connection to others that your yoga practice inspires then becomes another way of going more deeply into yoga itself by being present, deeply listening, and celebrating the unity that define us all.

SUGGESTED READING

Dass, Ram, and Bush, Mirabai. *Compasssion in Action: Setting Out on the Path of Service.* New York: Crown, 1995.

Dass, Ram, and Gorman, Paul. *How Can I Help? Stories and Reflections on Service.* New York: Knopf, 1985.

Creating Your Own Path

11.

As a novice to yoga, the process of beginning your practice might take the form of finding a class and a teacher that you are comfortable with. Or it may emerge at home as you set aside time to follow the instructions for postures in this and other books, or by watching videotapes. Learning the poses, becoming familiar with the breathing techniques, and acquainting yourself with the materials available about yoga are all part of developing a practice.

Thinking about how to stick with the practice is important as you begin. Like all good habits, it takes a while for the routine of yoga to become a natural part of your day, so you may need some pointers to support you. Here are some thoughts to consider as you approach bringing a yoga practice into your life:

"You must understand the whole of life, not just one little part of it. That is why you must read, that is why you must look at the skies, that is why you must sing, and dance, and write poems, and suffer, and understand, for all that is life."

—J. KRISHNAMURTI

- Be honest with yourself. If you have only ten minutes, find a routine that takes ten minutes and honor that. The combinations in Chapter 9 of this book are designed to fit many schedules.

- Create a space that is attractive and welcoming. Light a candle, burn some incense, keep the lights down low. Invite yourself in.

- Make it easy to practice. Set aside the same time every day—early mornings work well, but evenings are also fine. If you hate to miss appointments, consider this time an appointment with yourself. And be on time—you know how you hate to be kept waiting.

- If you practice in the evening or after work, you may want to begin with some restorative poses to let the stress of the day ease away and allow you to be more present with your practice. If you practice late at night before bed, you may want to avoid back bends or other stimulating postures. Work instead with postures that feel quiet and soothing.

- No matter how brief your practice time may be, start out with a moment of centering and warming up. Tune in to your energy level, scan your body for any sore or tense areas.

- Try not to eat two hours before practicing. If this is not possible, eat something light. And if you've had a regular meal, practice anyway. The rule about eating is to optimize your experience, but if you practice on a full belly you are not risking harm.

- Sign on the dotted line. If you find yourself procrastinating about your practice, write yourself a contract. You'll probably be less likely to ignore a written agreement than a mental one. Make it something you can agree to: yoga practice three mornings a week for two weeks, for example. If this method works, try it again.

- Set aside a moment or two after your practice to reflect on how you feel during this practice versus others. Can you sense where your tension is hiding today? How did the poses feel—has anything changed? Are your thoughts and emotions the same when you ended the practice as when you started?

- You may want to bring a journal to the mat, because sometimes thoughts emerge during practice that are worth keeping. Take a minute to record your feelings, insights, or dreams—or just jot down passing thoughts. This is another way to listen to your own voice.

- Support your success by creating realistic expectations. For example, setting a goal of completing one round of the Salutation to the Sun every other morning may be enough as you start out. Make it part of the goal to go beyond just performing a routine of postures. Listen to what your body wants and notice the feelings and sensations that emerge as you initiate your practice.

- Meet this goal, and then reflect on what you would like to add. You might want to explore more postures or to continue with the routine you've selected, but to go into it more deeply.

- On the seventh day, rest. Ideally, it is best to practice six days a week, but if you can't do this, don't worry. What matters most is that you have a regular practice, so if it is four days instead of six, enjoy those four. The quality of your practice is more important than the quantity.

- Most important, savor it. Breathe into the movements. Why set aside the time if you aren't going to experience it fully? Yoga is about the joy of being alive, the pleasure of using the body and nurturing the peace of a focused mind.

In addition to practicing in your class and at home, remember that yoga is one of your most portable tools. You can use the skills that you develop in yoga in small, subtle ways throughout the day.

"When I first began yoga, I lived on the surface of my personality. My physical self, which I considered to be my entire being, was easily tired, bored, and fragile. It was not enough for me. I wanted more: more life, more knowledge, more strength, more everything. I realized that I could not do it on my own and turned to my spiritual body to enlarge and brighten my world. It was a wonderful decision. My fragile physical nature turned inward to find the great power of my spiritual body waiting for me with open arms."

—ALICE CHRISTENSEN, *YOGA OF THE HEART*

"What a wonderful life I've had! I only wish I'd realized it sooner."

—COLETTE

+ Still the mind. When you're feeling distracted in a business meeting, for example, you can use a quiet breathing technique, concentrating on the steady in and out of your breath to bring your focus back to the present moment.

+ Listen to the body. Does your belly feel nervous as you walk into a meeting? Take a moment to acknowledge it, pause, and breathe into the feeling. And this is not only about listening to anxiety or discomfort. Next time your child brings home a test she scored well on, or you share a joke with a friend, or complete an art project to your satisfaction, tune into how your body feels. Are you aware of any physical sensations when you experience pride, or joy, or creative pleasure?

+ Celebrate the spirit. Whether it's the choice to share a smile, the pause you might take to appreciate the beauty of a fresh spring morning, or a gesture of kindness for no reason other than kindness, the spirit of yoga (remember—the word means "union") is about creating and experiencing connection. The connection is within ourselves, with others, and with nature. By opening yourself up to recognizing these moments, you bring a little yoga practice with you everywhere.

Here are two real-life examples to demonstrate how using your yoga practice as an overall path, or way of approaching situations, can make a real difference.

If you feel tension in your shoulders from working at a keyboard or driving, bring your awareness to this area of your body. What do you need to do?

When you're sitting at your keyboard and feeling stressed, you could accept the fact that you need to take a break and get up, walk around, and just loosen up. This may mean rolling your shoulders and neck, it may mean swinging your arms, perhaps it means resting your eyes. What really matters is that you listen to what you need—whether you are practicing yoga in the early-morning light or feeling pressure at work.

Or if you're driving and feel tense and tired, pull over and stand outside of the car

Yoga Notes

Have you ever kept a travel diary? If so, the itinerary it begins with may not be the journey that is described in the pages—which is exactly the nature of traveling.

Starting to practice yoga is like beginning on a journey. You may have one idea of where you're going, but along the way your interest may be sparked by taking another route, or your imagination may latch onto a totally new idea about where you are heading.

You may want to keep a notebook to record your expectations and changes and to help you explore the thoughts you have while developing your practice. In addition to your thoughts, here are some things you may want to reflect on by taking your yoga notes:

◆ Explore why you are starting to study yoga. For example, you might list the hopes and expectations you are bringing to your practice.

◆ Take a moment to think beyond the immediate benefit—that is, "a more toned body," or "less stress"—and also explore what these benefits may mean to you. In other words, what is the deeper impulse for starting yoga?

◆ Give yourself a chance to look at any reservations you have about yoga, as well. How do you feel about being a novice? Are you hesitant about being in a new group, or cautious about getting in touch with your body?

◆ As you begin to practice, note how you feel about the different poses. If a certain routine or a particular class left you feeling especially exhilarated or surprisingly sad, add that to your yoga notes.

◆ Reflect on the changes you see yoga bringing to your life off the mat.

for a moment, taking in the fresh air. Close your eyes. Give yourself a few minutes to go within. Hear what your body is telling you.

Both of these examples may seem overly simplistic. Since when is taking an office break or heading into a rest stop a way of doing yoga?

This is about more than taking a break. When you bring yoga into your everyday life, you may begin to listen to yourself more and make choices that honor what's best for you. In the first scenario, you could also walk away from your desk, pour a cup of coffee from a pot that has been sitting for hours, grab a doughnut from the box someone brought in that morning, and share a complaint with a colleague before getting back to your project. That's a common way to respond to office stress—but does it serve you in the long run? If you took a moment to check in with your wisest voice, is this what it would tell you to do?

Or, in the second scenario, you could get out of your car, wander into a fast food restaurant, buy a large cola and fries, and get back on the road. Whether you choose the first or second approach, you will get your project done on time and you will probably arrive at your destination safely.

But isn't there more to the choice? Could you complete your work project, but do

Singing, Really Singing

"We lead extremely busy lives. Even though we do not have to do as much manual labor as people in former times, we never seem to have enough time for ourselves. I know people who say they do not even have enough time to eat or breathe, and it appears to me to be true! What can we do about this? Can we take hold of time with both hands and slow it down?

"First, let us light the torch of our awareness and learn again how to drink tea, eat, wash dishes, walk, sit, drive and work in awareness. We do not have to be swept along by circumstances. We are not just a leaf or a log in a rushing river. With awareness, each of our daily acts takes on a new meaning, and we discover that we are more than machines, that our activities are not just mindless repetitions. We find that life is a miracle, the universe is a miracle and we too are a miracle.

"When we are invaded by confusion and dispersion, we can ask ourselves, 'What exactly am I doing right now? Am I wasting my life?' These questions immediately delight our awareness and return our attention to our breathing. A small smile naturally appears on our lips, and each second of our work becomes alive. If you want to sing, please sing! Really sing!"

—THICH NHAT HANH, *THE SUN MY HEART*

> "Yoga offers us a whole way of approaching our actions in the world. Action, after all, is a key element of life. There is no one who can escape acting. Our actions are significant, however, insofar as they as they either lead us into confusion and bondage, or into freedom. Some further our reintegration, while others do not. The difference rests in the state of mind with which we enter into the things we do.
>
> —A. G. MOHAN

so in such a way that you still have enough energy to enjoy your evening? Can you get to your destination safely and also emerge from the car with optimistic expectations for whatever comes next—instead of carrying the difficulty of a long drive in with you along with your overnight bag?

The difference between these two approaches is the fact that one approach is a conscious choice and one is more habitual. The increase in making conscious choices is a subtle part of practicing yoga, especially for beginners. Practicing yoga is, in part, about becoming aware of what you need, accepting it, and then honoring it. This is how being on the mat may begin to change your life in little ways.

Here's a heads-up: Once you begin to make choices that reflect your inner listening about the little things in your life—such as creating a work break in the office courtyard instead of the kitchenette—this same inner listening may begin to tune into the bigger questions in your life.

Staying on Track

Like everything, yoga has a honeymoon period. One day the bloom may fade from the lotus blossom. If the novelty wears off—and this could take three weeks or three years, as everyone is different—you may find that sometimes you resist going to class. You may find that errands, or work, or social commitments, or heading home to watch a TV show all seem much more important than yoga, even if you've paid for the class in advance. Or the ritual of lighting a few candles in your living room and pushing back the couch before you slip the Lilias Folan or Rodney Yee video in the VCR just seems like it's worn thin—and so has the practice itself. If this happens, it's a natural reaction. When you don't want to do yoga anymore, what should you do?

One possibility, of course, is to take a break. As you begin to make friends in your yoga class, you probably will meet people who started a few years ago, stopped, and then one day just decided to start again, and this time stuck with it. If you decide to step back for a while, that's fine. The lessons you learned on the mat can remain with you, so the benefits of deep breathing or the awareness of flexibility and balance can still be part of your life. Create an amicable break, because remaining friends with your yoga practice will serve you in the long run.

Another possibility is to tune in to what might be going on inside you that is being expressed as impatience or distraction. Remember, yoga is as much about listening to your inner voice as it is about awakening your body—even if that has not seemed obvious. As you've been exploring postures, bringing your focus to how the breath coordinates with movement, or playing with the "edge" of the stretch, you've also been training yourself to listen to your own voice. Many students, no matter how many weeks or months or years they've been at it, recognize the resistance to practice as an invitation to listen even more closely to the inner voice.

If you want to take a break, or if you are feeling uncomfortable with any practice at all, you may discover (by listening to your inner voice) that you have come upon one of the ironies of the practice. Yoga feels really good and can make you feel so healthy and strong that as you look around your life, you want to make some changes. And that impulse, that desire to make changes, is not always a welcome feeling.

As your body learns to relax and your mind finds the joys and clarity of stillness, you may acquire a renewed sensitivity to what is going on in your life. Many of the benefits of yoga—such as strength, flexibility, balance, and awareness—may initiate questions about your familiar habits.

"Wisdom is the ability to see life as it is, not the way I want it to be."

—CHARLOTTE JOKO BECK

This is because, like most people, you probably live a life based on certain ideas about what it means to be comfortable. Once you gain a heightened awareness of yourself, these ideas change. In other words, you may discover that situations that you found tolerable don't seem like healthy choices anymore. You may question what occupies your thoughts, what you eat, how you create your relationships.

This isn't magic, and it isn't therapy. It's just what happens as one becomes more in tune with the mind and body. All this means is that you may be doing what you came to yoga to do in the first place: changing. And though it might be expected that a new perspective is a joyous, life-giving shift (which it ultimately can be), it is also something many people are trained to resist.

Eric Shiffmann writes about the conflict between resistance and change in *Yoga: The Spirit and Practice of Moving Into Stillness.* He suggests that it has to do with an acceptance of one's own growth.

"In order to stay comfortable as you grow, you must flow with the changes and not attempt to remain the same—just as you buy a new pair of shoes for your son or daughter when their feet have outgrown the pair they've been wearing. It's not reasonable for them to continue wearing their favorite shoes when they no longer fit. You get rid of the old ones and buy a new pair. But the reason you need new ones is that their feet have grown. Growth has occurred. Their foot grew, the shoe became too small, their foot hurt. Pain is not an inherent part of being a foot. Nor is it an inherent part of growth.

"Your feet cannot be comfortable in a pair of shoes that has become too small . . . nor can you be comfortable in old belief structures and limited self concepts . . .

> "The purity of mind depends on the purity of food."
> —SWAMI SIVANANDA

you must let go of that which until now has been a protective coating or shield—and bloom. With the blooming will come a new sense of self and new appreciation for life."

This is a normal part of studying yoga. If you do feel pulled toward making changes in your life, remember to do so with compassion and loving kindness toward yourself. It is one thing to reject a behavior, a choice, or a habit, and it is another to make one's self "wrong."

This is why the idea of acceptance is so important. Just as the study of yoga can help initiate change, yoga also helps us to accept ourselves. This acceptance is a vital part of transformation. Without acceptance, the changes we make will remain on the surface.

You Are What You Eat

Though many of the changes yoga brings about are subtle, one of the areas of your life in which the impulse to change may show up is at your kitchen table.

People who have been studying yoga for a while—for some it may be a month, for others longer—begin to notice that they are more attracted to one kind of food than another. When they linger over a buffet table, they pile their plate with carrot sticks instead of minidogs. When the dessert cart rolls around, they eye the chocolate tort but choose the bowl of colorful fresh berries. First they notice how keyed up a second cup of coffee makes them feel, and then they stop drinking it. They might even replace Chardonnay with Perrier.

The practice of yoga awakens the body to what it really needs, honing the body's sensitivity to the fuel and nourishment that is best for keeping it healthy and energized. It's all part of the idea that what you learn in the yoga class is valid off the mat,

> "The foods which increase life, purity, strength, health, joy and cheerfulness, which are savory and oleaginous, substantial and agreeable, are dear to the sattvic people."
> —BHAGAVAD GITA, 17-8

as well. In terms of diet, that means the inner knowing you've cultivated from practicing the poses may be speaking up. Your wise inner voice may not want the sluggish feeling that a second mug of beer will leave you with, and now it wants to avoid the jagged rush of sugar.

Along with a new sensitivity to the negative reactions of some foods comes an enhanced delight from others. As you begin to feel more alive in your body, and as the yoga practice rejuvenates a sense of enthusiasm and confidence, foods that promote well-being begin to look more attractive. You may associate the light, vegetarian meal with feeling more energetic, or be satisfied with simple, low-fat snacks, shunning that pricey little bag of chips. The change will probably evolve slowly and feel as natural as scheduling time on a business trip to practice yoga in your hotel room.

The Yogic System of Food

Almost everything we buy today lists the amount of minerals, vitamins, protein, carbohydrates, fats, and other nutrients it contains. Labels tell us about "nutrition facts" or "minimal daily requirements."

There are other ways of understanding the effect of food choices on our health, however. The yogic scriptures divide food into three types: sattvic, or pure; rajasic, or stimulating; and tamasic, or impure and static.

According to this school of thought, sattvic foods promote health, vitality,

> "The foods that are bitter, sour, saline, excessively hot, pungent, dry and burning, are liked by the rajasic and are productive of pain, grief, and disease."
> —BHAGAVAD GITA, 17-9

> "That food which is stale, tasteless, putrid, rotten, and impure refuse,
> is the food liked by the tamasic."
> —BHAGAVAD GITA, 17-10

strength, and tranquility. They calm the mind and sharpen the intellect, maintaining mental poise throughout the day. They are also soothing and nourishing to the body. They include raw fruits and raw or lightly cooked vegetables, nuts, seeds, legumes, whole-grain bread, dairy products such as cheese and butter, and herbal tea. They are additive and chemical free.

Rajasic foods, on the other hand, put people into overdrive with excessive energy and agitation, leading to discomfort. They create a distracting, restless state of mind or might bring about a constant case of the jitters. Rajasic foods inhibit the possibility for the mind-body balance that is thought to be essential for happiness and may contribute to nervous disorders. Foods in a rajasic diet include stimulants such as onion, garlic, coffee, black tea, sugary foods (yes, even chocolate), and spicy and salted foods. Tobacco is also considered rajasic.

Tamasic foods contribute to lethargy, laziness, and inactivity. They are thought to increase feelings of laziness, decrease motivation and purpose, and are associated with depression. Overeating is also considered tamasic. Tamasic items are meat, fish, eggs, drugs and alcohol, as well as any foods that have been fermented, burned, fried, or re-heated many times. Mushrooms, because they grow in darkness, are also considered tamasic.

Yogis also believe that the food we eat reflects a level of mental purity and that preferences may change as one becomes more spiritually in tune. The kind of personality we have also impacts the category of food that would most benefit us. For example, if your personality matches the description of rajasic food, you might benefit from eliminating these foods from your diet, as they could be exacerbating a rajas nature.

> "It's not what you eat, it's what's eating you."

It will probably come as no surprise, therefore, that ancient teachings suggest the diet believed most likely to promote health, and that partners most agreeably with a yogic lifestyle, is sattvic. And anyone who has tried a diet of mostly vegetarian whole foods would most likely agree that the body begins to feel lighter and the mind is clearer when foods in the sattvic category are included in the diet.

It is useful to recognize how different qualities of food can contribute to our overall feeling, as well as to mental clarity. However, in today's world diet is understood to be more inclusive and comprehensive than when the yogis first developed this system. We now know that ethnic heritage and blood type play a role in the kinds of food our bodies need, as does the season, our stress level, physical activity and a myriad of other factors. We are more individual than this or any other system reflects, and we must listen to our bodies as we choose our foods.

This listening is exactly what will introduce improvements into your diet as you pursue your practice of yoga. You may not be inclined to become a vegetarian, and even if you already eat a healthful diet you may still keep your beloved cup of coffee and that occasional chewy cookie. This is also healthy, as "everything in moderation" is truly the most loving guidance of any diet.

When you tune into your inner "food choice voice," listen with the kind of attention you have learned to give your body on the mat, and you will most likely hear it asking for wholesome, fresh foods. You will be drawn to foods that make you feel alive, energized, and content. Enjoying healthful, delicious meals, served in a pleasant atmosphere, and shared with good friends—not gobbled down on the run—will become a natural choice. Bon appetit!

Meditation

In addition to toning the body and inspiring healthful behavior choices, the practice of yoga may introduce you to a sense of yourself that you want more of—that wonderful place of stillness where the mind is at rest and the heart feels happy. Blending meditation into your yoga practice can deepen this experience and expand the ways in which you experience a sense of spirituality and connection.

It may be interesting for beginners to note that meditation is not required in order to benefit from yoga. Nor do you have to be in a posture in order to mediate—in fact, you can mediate almost anywhere.

Practicing meditation is similar to learning the yogic breathing exercises. In those exercises, the mind is focused on the in-and-out rhythm of the breath. This is in part to still the mind and in part to train the body in these breathing techniques. Concentrating on the in-and-out of the breath is one useful meditation tool, but because the mind is not concentrating solely on stillness, learning yogic breathing techniques is not entirely a meditation practice.

The goal of meditation is to focus and quiet the mind. The point is to free the mind from the stream of thoughts that usually inhabit it. One reason to try meditation is simply to experience the rest that it provides to an overstimulated mind, offering the same kinds of physiological stress-reducing benefits that are associated with yoga. Another is the opportunity for a deeper sense of well-being.

How to Meditate

- ✦ Meditation is usually practiced in a quiet place, free from distractions.
- ✦ Find a comfortable seated position. Experiment with which is the most conducive for you: the Lotus or Cross-legged posture, sitting in a chair, or kneeling. Your spine and head should be erect.

> "Rest does not come from sleeping but from waking."
>
> —*A COURSE IN MIRACLES*

+ Rest your hands on your knees or thighs, palms down or palms up. Or position your hands on your knees, palms faceup and thumbs and index fingers joined.

+ Lower your gaze and regulate your breathing. Bring your thoughts to a specific point—it might be a sound, or your breath, or an image—and let your mind rest there.

+ The natural tendency of the mind is to hop from one interesting idea to another. Be prepared for this by having something to offer your mind so it can gravitate toward one consistent point rather than jumping around. Concentrate on the sound of your breath or on a self-nurturing affirmation.

+ When your mind wanders, gently bring it back to this point. It is more accustomed to being all over the place than it is to being focused, so be patient. Be kind to the mind.

+ Start out by meditating for five or ten minutes. You may want to tack it onto the end of your yoga practice.

Beginners to yoga may be surprised by this brief description. With all the books, workshops, and retreats that offer instruction in meditation, how can it be as simple as sitting down and letting the mind be free?

Rest assured that finding the degree of stillness that meditation ultimately can offer is not a simple task, primarily because the busy mind is not inclined to stop. The reason it is worth the energy it takes to tame the wild thoughts and the reason it partners so well with yoga is because of what one finds within one's self through the mindful quality of meditation.

"A mindful mind is like a mirror that is meticulously polished," write Joan Budilovsky and Eve Adamson in *The Complete Idiot's Guide to Yoga.* "It reflects what is really there and nothing else. When you become mindful, you learn to suspend everything you believe about yourself. Your limits, your shortcomings, your fears, what people have told you that you can and can't do—all these are put on hold. What's left is the real you, and your possibilities are limitless. Mindfulness takes courage. It can be scary to look at the real you. But if you take a good look, you'll have new power. You'll understand who you are like never before. And, as your self-concept expands, so will your concept of the world. Everything is within your grasp. Yet you aren't grasping—you're simply living, achieving, and being the best person you can possibly be."

Meditation can be taken off the cushion just as yoga is taken off the mat, they explain. "Once you've made meditation a part of your life, you can gradually learn to carry its principles with you throughout your day. When negative feelings arise, push

Meditation

Set aside some time to be with yourself in meditation. You can take yourself to a beautiful place outside, create a special meditation area in your home, or sit in the same chair you watch television from. *Where* you are does not matter as much as *how* you are: attentive, quiet, and open.

Give yourself a few minutes in the chair or on the cushion to settle in. Scan your body for areas of tension, letting them go with each breath. Give yourself a moment to feel relaxed, stable, and comfortable. Then bring your attention to your breath. Close your eyes and concentrate on the feel of breath filling you as you inhale, and draining from your body as you exhale.

Your mind may wander—everyone's does—so when this happens, gently bring it back to the rhythm of the breath. Many thoughts will bubble up and crowd your mind. Observe them, then let them drift away. Abide by the sensation of your breath.

If there is any part of you that feels closed, direct your breath to that area. Imagine bathing the area with warm, soothing light with every inhalation, and of softly relaxing the area—whether it is your heart, your belly, or your chattering mind—with each exhalation.

Allow watching the breath to bring you a feeling of calm and equanimity. When you are ready, slowly open your eyes, keeping the gaze soft. Move tenderly as you come to standing. Sink into the grounded, centered feel of your feet against the floor, and observe how quiet your body feels. Savor this peace as you make the transition from meditation practice to the rest of the day.

them away as if they were balloons. If people are unkind, unfair, or judgmental of you, you can learn gently to push these balloons away, too. Meditation in daily life means remembering the peace and stillness you've learned to achieve during regular meditation, then finding that peace and stillness throughout the day. The real you will shine best when you're in touch with the inner peace."

Bringing the practice of yoga into your daily life may mean that you gain access to the joy and light that is already within you, right now, even as you read this page. The practice may also bring about changes that are challenging, even uncomfortable. This is all part of the practice. As you deepen your experience on the mat, you will be allowing yourself to respond to these changes in a living, positive way.

SUGGESTED READING

Cleary, Thomas (trans.). *Buddhist Yoga: A Comprehensive Course.* Boston: Shambhala, 1995.

Hanh, Thich Nhat. *The Blooming of a Lotus: Guided Meditation and Yoga as Christian Spiritual Practice.* Boston: Beacon Press, 1997.

Hanh, Thich Nhat. *The Long Road Turns to Joy: A Guide to Walking Meditation.* Berkeley, Ca.: Parallax, 1996.

Hanh, Thich Nhat. *The Miracle of Mindfulness: A Manual on Meditation.* Boston: Beacon, 1995.

Hewitt, James. *The Complete Yoga Book: Yoga of Breathing, Yoga of Posture, and Yoga of Meditation.* New York: Schocken Books, 1990.

Knaster, Mirka. *Discovering the Body's Wisdom.* New York: Bantam, 1996.

Kornfield, Jack. *A Path with Heart: A Guide Through the Perils and Promises of Spiritual Life.* New York: Bantam, 1993.

Kornfield, Jack. *Buddhism in the West: Spiritual Wisdom for the 21st Century.* Carlsbad, Ca.: Hay House, 1998.

Kriyananda, Sri. *The Path: One Man's Quest on the Only Path There Is.* Nevada City, Ca.: Crystal Clarity, 1996.

Ryan, Thomas. *Prayer of Heart and Body: Meditation and Yoga as Christian Spiritual Practice.* New York: Paulist Press, 1995.

Walton, Todd. *Open Body: Creating Your Own Yoga.* New York: Avon, 1998.

Conclusion

As you develop your practice, remember to honor and celebrate the decision that brought you to yoga in the first place. No matter what inspired you—the advice of a doctor, the suggestion of a friend, basic curiosity, or an inner knowing that recognized the nurturing and insights that yoga will offer—it is a decision that is self-loving and courageous. The study of yoga can create positive change not only in your body but emotionally and spiritually, as well. Your choice to initiate these changes was a wise one.

The true purpose of yoga is to unify—to yoke or join our selves with the Divine, or Universal Energy, that courses through all living things. This experience of connection is brought to life through yoga by unifying the mind, body, and spirit. The greatest benefits of the practice are realized when each part of the self is working together, allowing you to feel healthier and more at peace.

"People say that what we're all seeking is a meaning for life. . . . I think that what we're really seeking is an experience of being alive, so that our life experiences on the purely physical plane will have resonance within our innermost being and reality, so that we can actually feel the rapture of being alive."

—JOSEPH CAMPBELL

Once you experience the deep listening and feeling of oneness in yoga, you know that it is possible—in fact, that it is probable—to evoke it in every area of your life. To have the knowledge that your life can feel this rewarding, this authentic, and this full of grace on a day-to-day basis is what allows yoga to come alive within you, your relationships, and in community.

General Resources

Birch, Beryl Bender. *Power Yoga: The Total Strength and Flexibility Workout.* New York: Simon & Schuster, 1995.

Budilovsky, Joan, and Adamson, Eve. *The Complete Idiot's Guide to Yoga.* New York: Macmillan, 1997.

Carrico, Mara (ed.). *Yoga Journal's Yoga Basics.* New York: Holt, 1997.

Chodron, Pema. *Start Where You Are: A Guide to Compassionate Living.* Boston: Shambhala, 1994.

Choudhury, Bikram. *Bikram's Beginning Yoga Class.* New York: Jeremy P. Tarcher, 1978.

Feuerstein, Georg, and Bodian, Stephan, with the staff of *Yoga Journal. Living Yoga: A Comprehensive Guide for Daily Life.* New York: Jeremy P. Tarcher, 1993.

Knaster, Mirka. *Discovering the Body's Wisdom.* New York: Bantam, 1996.

Kornfield, Jack. *A Path with Heart: A Guide Through the Perils and Promises of Spiritual Life.* New York: Bantam, 1993.

Kripalu Yoga Fellowship. *The Self-Health Guide.* Lenox, Mass.: Kripalu Publishers, 1980.

Lasater, Judith. *Relax and Renew: Restful Yoga for Stressful Times.* Berkeley, Ca.: Rodmell, 1995.

Mohan, A. G., and Miller, Kathleen (eds.). *Yoga for Body, Breath, and Mind: A Guide to Personal Reintegration.* Cambridge, Mass.: Rudra, 1995.

Myers, Esther. *Yoga and You: Energizing and Relaxing Yoga for New and Experienced Students.* Boston: Shambhala, 1997.

Rama, Swami, Ballentine, Rudolph, and Hymes, Alan. *Science of Breath.* Hinesdale, Pa.: Himalayan Institute, 1979.

Schaeffer, Rachel. *Yoga for Your Spiritual Muscles.* Wheaton, Ill.: Quest Books, 1998.

Schiffmann, Erich. *Yoga: The Spirit and Practice of Moving Into Stillness.* New York: Pocket Books, 1996.

WEB SITES

www.yoga.com
A variety of articles and products, links to other yoga pages.

www.spiritweb.org
A great description of different approaches to yoga.

www.drweil.com
A great resource for beginners interested in the body-mind connection. Includes "Ask Dr. Weil" and subject-driven links to other sites.

www.thriveonline.com
An overview of health and fitness research in an easy-to-access format.

www.healthynet.com
Includes valuable studies and articles on mind-body research.

altmed.od.nih.gov
The Web page for the National Center for Complementary and Alternative Medicine at the National Institutes of Health. Includes a regularly updated database of studies and articles.

A Beginner's Yoga Glossary

adho mukha shvanasana   Downward Facing Dog; a forward bend

ahimsa   One of the *yamas*; nonviolence

Ananda yoga   A school of yoga that teaches specific affirmations, or positive thoughts, to accompany different poses

anuloma viloma   A breathing exercise in which nostrils are alternated for inhalation and exhalation

apana   A type of *prana*; the vital energy of excretion that flows downward and out of the body, ridding it of impurities

aparigraha   One of the *yamas*; nongreed

ardha matsyendrasana   The Seated Twist; a twisting pose

asanas   The postures, or exercises, of yoga, designed to help you master control of your own body

Ashtanga yoga   Literally referring to the eight limbs of yoga, this has come to mean a Hatha yoga practice that includes an intense *vinyasa* workout

asteya   One of the *yamas*; nonstealing

baddha konasana   The Butterfly; a sitting posture

Bikram yoga   A school of yoga using heat and a high-energy workout

Bhagavad Gita   One of India's most beloved and famous sacred texts, it is the epic story of Arjuna, a warrior prince, who confronts moral dilemmas and is led to a better understanding of reality through the intercession of the god Krishna

Bhakti yoga   Sincere, heartfelt devotion to the Divine is the primary focus of this type of yoga

bhramari   Also known as Bee Breath, this breathing technique imitates the sound of a bee

bhujangasana   The Cobra pose; a back bend

brahmacharya   One of the *yamas*; continence and self-respect with regard to indulgence in sexual pleasure

brahman   The Absolute, or Divinity Itself

buddhi   The intellect

chakras   Centers of energy that exist between the base of your spinal column and the crown of your head

dhanurasana   The Bow pose; a back bend

dharana   The sixth limb of yoga, the practice of concentration

dhyana   The seventh limb of yoga in which one experiences stillness of the mind

gunas   A system of three catagories used in yoga to define the nature of the material world: sattvas, of the nature of purity; rajas, of the nature of passion; tamas, of the nature of dullness

guru   A spiritual teacher

halasana   The Plough; an inversion

Hatha yoga   A type of yoga primarily concerned with control over the physical body as a path to enlightenment; combines opposing forces to achieve balance

Integral yoga   A school of yoga based on the teachings of Swami Satchidananda

ishvara-pranidhana   One of the *niyamas*; centering on the divine

Iyengar yoga   A school of yoga that follows the teachings of B. K. S. Iyengar and focuses on alignment and technique.

janusirasana   Sitting one leg; a forward bend

Jnana yoga   This type of yoga emphasizes questioning, meditation, and contemplation as paths to enlightenment

kapalabhati   A cleansing ritual for the respiratory tract, lungs, and sinuses; also called skull shining

karma   The law of cause and effect, or the movement toward balanced consciousness; everything you do, say, or think has an immediate effect and will reverberate back to you in some way

Karma yoga   Selfless action and service to others

Kripalu yoga   A school of yoga developed by Yogi Amrit Desai and named after Swami Kripalu, a great Indian yogi and the guru of Yogi Desai.

kundalini   A psychospiritual energy force in the body that is often compared to a snake lying curled at the base of the spine, waiting to be awakened

Kundalini yoga   A form of yoga centered around awakening and employing kundalini energy

mantra   A sound or sounds that resonate in the body and evoke certain energies during meditation

matsyasana   The Fish pose; a back bend

mudhasana   The Child's pose; a forward bend

mudras   Hand gestures that direct the life current through the body

namaste mudra   A *mudra* in which the hands are placed together in prayerlike fashion to honor the inner light

niyamas   Five observances or personal disciplines, as defined by Patanjali in his *Yoga Sutras*; the *niyamas* are *shauca, santosha, tapas, svadhyaya,* and *ishvar-pranidhana*

om   A sacred syllable commonly used as a *mantra* during meditation and representative of the absolute or oneness of the universe

padmasana   The Lotus pose, a meditative posture in which the legs are crossed and each foot is placed on the opposite thigh; the pose is said to resemble the perfection of the lotus flower

prana   A form of energy in the universe that animates all physical matter, including the human body and the vital energy of respiration

pranayama   Breathing exercises designed to help you master control of your breath

pratyahara   The fifth limb of yoga, the practice of drawing inside of oneself

Raja yoga   Also known as the Royal Path, it is a type of yoga that emphasizes control of the intellect to attain enlightenment

rajas   The quality of high activity and agitation; a *guna*

Rig-Veda   Literally "Knowledge of Praise," the Rig-Veda consists of 1,028 hymns and is the oldest known reference to yoga, and possibly the oldest known text in the world

samadhi   The eighth limb of yoga; the state of meditation in which ego disappears and all becomes one

santosha   One of the *niyamas*; contentment

sarvangasana   The Full Shoulder Stand; an inversion

satya   One of the *yamas*; truthfulness

sethu bandhasana   The Bridge pose; an inversion

saucha   One of the *niyamas*; purity, or inner and outer cleanliness

shavasana   Also known as the Corpse pose, this pose is meant to bring the body and mind into total, conscious relaxation

sirsasana   The Headstand; an inversion

sitali   A breathing technique involving rolling the tongue, then inhaling through it like a straw; a cooling technique

Sivananda yoga A school of yoga that teaches a five-point philosophy, including breath, relaxation, diet, exercise, and positive thinking.

sukhasana Cross-legged posture; a meditative pose

surya namaskara Salutation to the Sun; a *vinyasa*

svadhyaya One of the *niyamas*; the process of inquiring into your own nature, the nature of your beliefs, and the nature of the world's spiritual journey

swami The Anglicized form of *svamin*, an iterant monk who has taken vows of renunciation of the worldly life; sometimes used as an honorific for someone of spiritual attainment

Swami Vivekananda A guru from India who addressed the Parliament of Religions in 1893

tadasana The Mountain pose; a standing posture

Tantra yoga A type of yoga characterized by certain rituals designed to awaken the *kundalini*

tapas One of the *niyamas*; self-discipline

trikonasana The Triangle or happy pose; a standing posture

ujjayi A breathing exercise that produces sound in the throat with the inhalation; literally, "she who is victorious"

Upanishads Scriptures of ancient Hindu philosophy

ustrasana The Camel pose; a back bend

Viniyoga A school of yoga that adjusts teaching to the level and needs of the students

vinyasa A steady flow of connected yoga *asanas* linked with breath work in a continuous movement; a particularly dynamic form of yoga

virabhadrasana The Warrior pose; a standing posture

virasana The Hero pose; a sitting posture

vrikshasana The Tree pose; a balance posture

yamas Five abstinences that purify the body and mind, as defined by Patanjali in his *Yoga Sutras*; the *yamas* are *ahimsa, satya, asteya, brahmacharya,* and *aparigraha*

Yoga Mudra A forward bend

Yoga Sutras of Patanjali The source of Patanjali's Eightfold Path, this collection of succinct aphorisms has largely defined the modern concept of yoga

Yogi An accomplished male student of yoga

Yogini An accomplished female student of yoga

Index

G

Gandhi, Mahatma, 16
Gerson, Hank, 159–161

H

Half Moon Pose—Ardha Chandrasana, 102–103
Half Shoulder Stand—Ardha Sarvangasana, 141–142
Happy, Healthy, Holy Organization (3HO), 41
Hara point, 105
Harris, Sidney J., 24
Hatha yoga, 8, 14 (*see also* Yoga)
    awareness and, 13
    benefits of, 12
    flexibility and, 13
    literal translation of *hatha*, 12–13, 33
    strength and endurance and, 13
Headstand—Sirasana, 145–146
Head to Knee—Janushirshasana, 122–123
Heart disease, 24, 28
Heart rate, 27
Hero Pose—Virasana, 140
Herschel, Rabbi Abraham, 59, 165
Hittleman, Richard, 9–10
Hurley, Suzi, 60, 63
Hypertension, 24, 27

I

Immune system, 26, 27
India, 6, 7
Integral yoga, 34, 40
International Congress of Religious Liberals, 8

Inversions
    Full Shoulder Stand—Sarvangasana, 143
    Half Shoulder Stand—Ardha Sarvangasana, 141–142
    Headstand—Sirasana, 145–146
    Plough—Halasana, 23, 58, 143–144
Isis Unveiled (Blavatsky), 8
Isvara-pranidhana (surrender to higher power), 55
Iyengar, B.K.S., 12, 34, 39
Iyengar yoga, 38–39

J

James, William, 165
Jet-lag Tune-up Routine, 155–156
Jnana yoga, 16
Jois, K. Pattabhi, 38
Jones, Jennifer, 9
Jung, Carl, 109

K

Kahn, Hazrat Inayat, 98
Kapalabhati—Skull Shining, 80
Karma yoga, 14, 15
Kesey, Ken, 14
King, Martin Luther, Jr., 16
King of the Dancers—Natrajanasana, 114–115
Knee Down Twist, 96–97
Kneeling Yoga Mudra, 124–125
Knee to Chest Pose—Apanasana, 94–97
Kornfield, Jack, 125
Kraftsow, Gary, 36
Kripalu, Swami, 16